FLORIDA
COCKTAILS

An Elegant Collection of over 100 Recipes Inspired by the Sunshine State

CARRIE HONAKER

CIDER MILL PRESS

BOOK
PUBLISHERS

FLORIDA COCKTAILS

ISBN-13: 978-1-40034-896-1
ISBN-10: 1-40034-896-X

This book may be ordered by mail from the publisher. Please include $5.99 for postage and handling. Please support your local bookseller first!

Books published by Cider Mill Press Book Publishers are available at special discounts for bulk purchases in the United States by corporations, institutions, and other organizations. For more information, please contact the publisher.

Cider Mill Press Book Publishers
"Where good books are ready for press"
501 Nelson Place
Nashville, Tennessee 37214
cidermillpress.com

Typography: Bodega Sans, Copperplate, Sackers, Warnock

Photography credits on page 279

Printed in India

25 26 27 28 29 REP 5 4 3 2 1

First Edition

CONTENTS

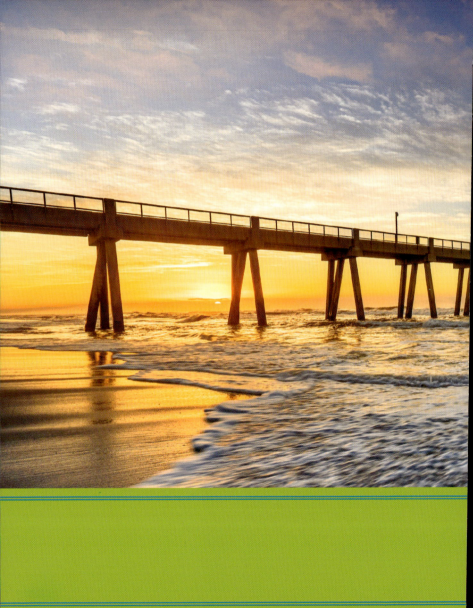

INTRODUCTION

Florida has its own mythology—the Skunk Ape roaming forests, mermaids swimming in crystal-clear springs, a town called Cassadaga that's filled with spiritualists and mediums, the Florida Man meme. And there's also its unique mix of environments—the Everglades, a swampy Shangri-la known to be one of the most biodiverse ecosystems in the world; the coastal dune lakes on 30A, an ecological wonder only found in four countries; and snow-colored sand filled with enough quartz from the Appalachian Mountains that it doesn't get hot and squeaks when you walk on it.

Florida is filled with the weird and wonderful, and the cocktail scene leans into that with its history of bootlegging and rum-running, a bounty of ingredients grown in the Sunshine State, and pioneering bartenders committed to fun and delicious drinks and excited to experiment with new techniques.

Blenders, Bikers, and Sandy Floors: Florida's Beach Bar Culture

"The great beach bar is somewhere where you just feel comfortable wandering in off the beach," says Jena Ellenwood, Florida native and award-winning bartender. "Maybe there's still some sand on the floor. It's open-air. There are some good snacks. There's usually some good music, interesting tchotchkes, maybe some bumper stickers, and it just feels like an extension of your beach trip."

Florida is predominantly an easy-drinking state.

Blenders at first, then, in the 1990s, frozen Daiquiri machines, usually made by Island Oasis, set the tone for Florida's cocktail scene. After a day in the surf or on the boat fishing, you could catch one of Florida's cotton-candy sunsets while relaxing with a drink. At some beach bars even today, you can boat up and tie into, like Snook Inn on Marco Island. The kitschier the better. For some beach bars, like Boot Hill Saloon on Daytona Beach, a biker bar culture took hold. Harley Davidson and Indian motorcycles line the parking lots, leather is the uniform, and stiff drinks are king.

In 1983, Hooters opened its flagship neighborhood restaurant and bar in Clearwater Beach, and if you grew up in Florida, you probably have a T-shirt or onesie (like Ellenwood) with their signature phrase, "More than a Mouthful," emblazoned on the front.

In 2015, Karen and Greg Darby took inspiration from their backyard bar and started Cruisin' Tikis in Fort Lauderdale. The concept is a floating tiki bar that accommodates up to six people and cruises around on the water while serving up cocktails. Places like Crab Island (more a state of mind than an island) in Destin's harbor takes inspiration from this concept, except people raft up together to create a bar island on the water.

The cocktail renaissance took hold in the early 2000s, and bartenders returned to the craft of mixology, employing fresh juices, layered techniques, and leaning on recipes from the golden age of Tiki. Still tropical, still refreshing, but more mindfully crafted.

Weathering Storms of All Kinds

All across Florida, people brace for hurricanes from June through November.

Alexa Delgado, now bar director at The Miami Beach EDITION hotel, was only a year and a half old when Hurricane Andrew, a Category 5, ripped through Miami in 1992. Many homes were destroyed, and in the aftermath, stray animals wandered the streets and papayas, avocados, and mangoes lay scattered across the sidewalks from lev-

eled farmlands. And there was no power. Then there was Hurricane Katrina in 2005, a Category 3, when the power was out for almost two weeks, a situation that would be repeated with Hurricane Irma in 2017. Still, somebody always has a generator, and somebody else has a gas stove. Somebody has coffee or hot dogs. And somebody has rum.

"We all take care of each other," says Delgado. "My family might do breakfast on the grill while the boys down the street cut up fallen trees with their chainsaws so we can get out of the neighborhood—it's the literal calm after the storm, gathering together," Delgado says. "You know you will lose power, but you get prepared for a night of board games and a good cocktail."

Floridians take the storms in stride, pour a drink, and rebuild with what is left. Florida's beach bars "refuse to let a hurricane wipe them away," says Jena Ellenwood.

In 2020, the pandemic brought its own wave of change to Florida's cocktail scene. To take the socializing outdoors, bartenders and forward-thinking bar owners flocked to the beach. Inventive and ambitious bar programs popped up around the state. Florida ingredients took center stage as this new generation figured out how to tell the story of this sun-soaked, oft-maligned state in a glass in a way that felt welcoming and unpretentious.

Punch Is Back

It is said that seventy-six bowls of punch were drunk at the signing of the Declaration of Independence. But punch—the boozy kind anyway—fell by the wayside as times changed and people had less time to sit around leisurely sharing a bowl of punch.

When seventeenth-century British sailors ran out of beer and wine, punch became a cocktail of necessity to get them through their long voyages. Sailors would combine spirits they came across with lemon juice, sugar, and water,  the citrus keeping scurvy at bay. When they docked, they would mix up a bowl of this punch to share with visitors while telling sea stories.

Punch became the cocktail of choice, and punch bowls became statement pieces in refined homes. When England colonized sugar-producing nations, rum became the star of the punch. According to cocktail historian Dave Wondrich's book *Punch: The Delights (and Dangers) of the Flowing Bowl*, "It became the drink for distilled spirits in every corner of the world in the 1600s and set up all the patterns mixed drinks have fallen into since. The Daiquiri, the Margarita, and anything that combines citrus, sugar, and spirits can trace its lineage back to punch."

And now punch is back and having a moment.

At Cane & Barrel in St. Petersburg, the cocktail program draws inspiration from a cocktail form that hails from the Age of Discovery and adds a modern resonance. Joel Valencia, food and beverage manager, says their version is "a celebration of the rich heritage of Florida. Our punch bowls blend a variety of tropical fruits and spices common in Hispanic cultures who made their mark in this area. It's not just a drink; it's an experience to share with friends and family, like you do around the table in Puerto Rico, Mexico, Cuba, and the Dominican Republic."

Florida's Troubadour: Jimmy Buffett

It's hard to untangle Key West and Jimmy Buffett. The troubadour fell in love with the Conch Republic when he landed there in 1971, and the island infused every song he wrote, drawing legions of fans to the laid-back beach lifestyle his music evoked. Key West became synonymous with Buffett and his armies of Parrotheads.

The Chart Room was Buffett's first stop in town, and according to Tom Corcoran's book, *Jimmy Buffett: The Key West Years*, he kept coming back to the lit-

Jimmy Buffett in 1981

tle-known bar hidden in The Pier House hotel at the end of Duval Street. He performed regularly in exchange for free drinks to audiences rumored to include writers Hunter S. Thompson, Truman Capote, Tennessee Williams, Shel Silverstein, and fellow musician Jim Croce. Buffett memorialized the bar in two songs: "Tin Cup Chalice" and "A Pirate Looks at Forty."

Buffett played at many other locations around Key West, collecting stories and characters that fueled his songwriting, but in 1977 he released a song that would become his biggest hit. "Margaritaville" became the siren call of bargoers everywhere to raise their glasses and sing along.

How to Drink Like a Floridian

- Put your toes in the sand and get a cool, refreshing cocktail in your hand.
- Find a body of water of any size and just be on "island time."
- Remember, you can't drink all day if you don't start in the morning (though be wary of "Florida Man/Woman" issues with this one . . .).
- Have a cocktail on the beach at sunset if you're there at sunrise, see above.
- Have a *cantinero*-style rum drink at a hip, palm tree–adorned bar, be it in Miami, Tampa, or your home.
- Create an Epcot Center of cocktails in honor of our wide-ranging international cocktail culture.
- Grab a few friends and be pirates for a day—enjoy rum-based cocktails aboard boat. Remember to elect a designated sober captain if you get the boat underway.
- Get yourself rafted up in the ocean, in the Gulf, in a gin-clear spring, or in any body of water large or small—with rafts, tubes, or boats at a tie-up.
- Absolutely try tropical cocktails from a floating tiki bar.
- Finally, remember, as Florida Artists Hall-of-Famer Jimmy Buffet famously sang, "It's Five O'Clock Somewhere."

Techniques and Preparations

Double Strain: Most cocktails in this book require just a single strain through a Hawthorne strainer (if using a shaking tin) or a julep strainer (if using a mixing glass). For the ones that call for a double strain, place a fine-mesh strainer over the glass, and pour the mixture through your Hawthorne or julep strainer through the mesh. This removes finer particles and pesky ice chips.

Create a Sugar, Salt, or Tajín Rim: Place the sugar or salt into a small saucer. Take your citrus wedge and rotate around the rim of the glass. Dip the rim into sugar, salt, or Tajín.

Express Citrus: Cut a peel of citrus and twist it over the drink. This releases the oils and aroma into your cocktail. Some drinks say to then add the peel as a garnish, while others may say to discard the peel.

Make Simple Syrup: Whitney Hobbs and Rob Crabtree, the geniuses behind Boat Drinks in St. Augustine, shared this recipe: combine 6 oz. sugar and 6 oz. filtered water, at room temperature, and blend in a blender until the sugar is dissolved. To make a rich simple syrup, double the sugar. To make a semi-rich version, use 1½ times the amount of sugar.

Make Saline Solution: Some recipes in the book call for this concoction. Award-winning bartender Chris Trull offered up this recipe: Add 20 grams Maldon Sea Salt Flakes to 2⅔ oz. (80 ml/80 grams) water, and stir until the salt is fully incorporated. Add the solution to a dropper bottle or dasher so you can then add it to cocktails a drop at a time.

Fat-Washing a Spirit

In 2007, Don Lee's Benton's Old Fashioned lit a fire around the cocktail world. The now-famed bartender, working at Please Don't Tell in New York, used bacon fat rendered from Benton's Smoky Mountain Country Ham to "wash" Four Roses Bourbon, and the result was a smoother, creamier finish with layers of flavor. Today, fat-washing—adding fat, whether from meat- or plant-based sources, to a spirit, freezing it overnight, then straining off the solids the next day—is a ubiquitous mixology move. The good news is, it's very doable for home mixologists as well.

You'll need a wide-neck freezer-safe container with a lid, a coffee filter for fine straining, and the fat and spirit you want to infuse. The ratio of fat to spirit is generally is 1:4. Depending on the fat, you may need to melt it in a saucepan. From there, you combine the spirit and fat and shake vigorously to ensure it combines. Freeze for at least two hours, but overnight is better. When finished, skim off the solidified fat and then strain the remainder through a coffee filter into a clean container, or better yet, back into the original bottle. Use now or refrigerate for up to one week, depending on fat. The flavor degrades over time, so fresher is better.

"Rolling" a Cocktail

Shaken, stirred, blended—these techniques are probably familiar to you if you've done any cocktail mixing, but one method you may not know is rolling a drink.

Rolling involves passing ingredients back and forth between two mixing glasses or shaker tins to chill and aerate the cocktail while also mixing the ingredients together. It is a gentler way to mix a cocktail, keeping it from forming bubbles. It's great for Bloody Marys, for example, to maintain the texture of the tomato juice while still diluting and chilling the beverage.

The technique is easy. Fill one shaker or mixing glass with ice and cover it with a fine-mesh strainer. Then fill another container with all of the ingredients for the cocktail. Slowly pour the ingredients into the shaker/mixing glass, through the strainer. Pass the liquid back and forth five or six times to chill and aerate the cocktail.

Once you've achieved the consistency you're looking for, pour the chilled cocktail into whatever glassware the recipe calls.

How to Set Up a Florida Home Bar

You bought the book, so now it's time to stock your bar with all the tools and ingredients you'll need to recreate the recipes found in the coming pages. Under Spirits and Such, I've provided the heavy hitters, but you may need some specialty items for just one or two recipes. Be sure to check out the Florida Distilleries section for great spirits produced here in the Sunshine State. Many of the recipes rely on fresh Florida citrus and produce. Just be sure to make a list before you head out shopping.

Tools

- Jigger
- Cocktail shaker
- Hawthorne strainer
- Julep strainer
- Mixing glass
- Fine-mesh strainer
- Muddler
- Blender

- Peeler/zester
- Paring knife
- Barspoon
- Cocktail picks
- Glassware
- Acrylic glassware for the pool and beach

- Juice reamer (you could also use a citrus press or juicer)
- Ice cube tray
- Tongs

Spirits and Such

- Rum—as much and as many varieties as you have room for
- Vodka
- Gin
- Mezcal
- Tequila
- Bourbon
- Crème de cocoa
- Kahlúa
- Aperol
- Angostura bitters
- Elderflower liqueur
- Coconut liqueur
- Banana liqueur
- Canned pineapple juice
- Ginger beer
- Coconut cream
- Tajín

Optional (not really)

- Palm trees—plastic, fabric, blow-up, real, it doesn't matter
- Pool—large, small, kiddie, inflatable, plastic, just something wet
- Fifty-pound bag of sugar-white sand
- Pirate flag
- Flamingo statues—without flamingos, is it even Florida?

Florida Playlist

The Florida cocktail experience would not be the same without some great tunes spinning. Mike Ragsdale, the founder of the 30A brand and lifestyle, found his oasis on an undeveloped stretch of Florida's Emerald Coast, left his corporate job, and became the visionary behind those little blue and yellow bumper stickers that capture his motto, "Life Shines on 30A." His musical taste is impeccable, so of course I tapped him to develop this playlist. "Like a well-paired wine or cocktail, the right song can amplify the moment, making every sunset and every wave a little more vivid; a little more unforgettable," Mike says.

"Holiday" by The Hip Abduction

"The Sound of Sunshine" by Michael Franti & Spearhead

"Mexico" by James Taylor

"We're The Tide" by Giants' Nest

"Summer Nights" by Van Halen

"Three Little Birds" by Bob Marley and the Wailers

"Mexicoma" by James T. Slater

"Havaña Daydreamin'" by Jimmy Buffett

"All Night" by Damien Marley and Stephen Marley

"Southern Cross" by Crosby, Stills, Nash & Young

Mike Ragsdale

FLORIDA ICONS

NAREN YOUNG, SWEET LIBERTY DRINKS & SUPPLY COMPANY

Naren Young, the creative director for Sweet Liberty Drinks & Supply Company in Miami, found his way to Florida after his close friend John Lermayer, the genius behind Sweet Liberty, died suddenly. Lermayer's partners reached out to Young, hoping he would come help steer the ship.

"John was such a big figure in this industry and an important person for many people, myself included," Young says. "On my third trip back to Miami, it started growing on me. New York is amazing, but it's full-on. After fifteen years, I thought maybe it was time to go somewhere more relaxed."

Young started in the hospitality industry in Australia at fourteen, vacuuming restaurants. He went on to run some of the better bars there, moved to London for a stint, and then moved to New York in 2006. He didn't know anybody but wanted to be in the epicenter of cocktail culture. "I became a bit of a student," he says, "learning from the best people, reading the books, and that culminated in Death & Co. Bar, which won a ton of awards and helped reshape what a restaurant bar could be."

His first move at Sweet Liberty was to balance simplicity, keeping signature drinks that people came for and that meshed with Miami's tropical heat, with an ambitious cocktail program. Then he worked on enhancing the experience. "I put a lot of effort into training, and it's really important to me that a culture [of hospitality] permeates through the whole place. That comes with helping your staff, mentoring them, and asking what they need."

Playful and not too serious while developing recipes, but with a lot of thought on the back end, remains Young's approach to mixology. An Apple Martini comes to life with an entire apple freshly juiced, the addition of calvados (French apple brandy), and apple cider vinegar—layers and layers, resulting in a cocktail experience that is like biting into a fresh Granny Smith apple.

The Sweet Liberty team opened another bar with Young as full partner, Medium Cool, in South Beach. Jazz lounge by day, it transforms into a nightclub later in the evening. Young's most recent project, The Regent Cocktail Club, serves as "a bit of a nursery to some of the top talent in the city." Also on the horizon is the Zebra Club—Martini trolleys, double-breasted velvet jackets, high-end glassware, and Young himself back behind the bar, serving up magic.

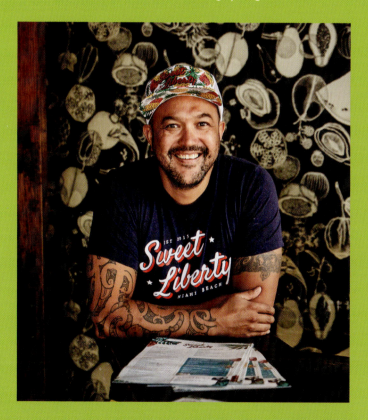

THE FLORIDA COCKTAIL

SWEET LIBERTY DRINKS & SUPPLY COMPANY
237 20TH STREET SUITE B, MIAMI BEACH

Looking through *The Fine Art of Mixing Drinks* by David A. Embury, first published in 1948, Naren Young found The Florida Cocktail. He reworked the recipe with his signature fluffy juice method, added green crème de menthe for a touch of color; rum, lime, and saline solution. "It's stunning. It's super crushable. It screams Florida," Young says. He developed his fluffy juice technique in New York while playing with his Garibaldi cocktail. He put the orange juice in a high-speed Breville juicer which helped aerate the juice, creating a light, frothy texture. Fluffy juices can be created at home using an immersion blender or a high-speed regular blender.

GLASSWARE: Collins glass
GARNISH: Mint sprig

- 1½ oz. Bacardí Añejo Cuatro
- ¼ oz. crème de menthe
- ¼ oz. fresh lime juice
- 3 dashes Saline Solution (see recipe on page 14)
- Fluffy Pineapple Juice (see recipe), to top

1. Freeze a collins glass. Combine all of the ingredients, except for the juice, in the frozen glass over 3 ice cubes.
2. Fill the glass halfway with Fluffy Pineapple Juice.
3. Stir again and top with more pineapple juice, then garnish with mint.

FLUFFY PINEAPPLE JUICE: Using a juicer machine or a blender and fine-mesh strainer, juice a pineapple. Then place the fresh pineapple juice in a high-speed blender (or use an immersion blender) and blend until the juice has a frothy texture.

THE SPANIARD

SWEET LIBERTY DRINKS & SUPPLY COMPANY
237 20TH STREET SUITE B, MIAMI BEACH

Naren Young's favorite cocktail on the menu at Sweet Liberty is The Spaniard, a riff on a Martini using Spanish ingredients such as manzanilla sherry and Licor 43. "It's this beautiful, complex Martini, which we serve straight from the freezer. It's always nice and cold," Young says. "I wanted each layer in there to be very subtle so you can taste them all, but nothing's overpowering, just perfect complexity."

GLASSWARE: Etched martini glass

GARNISH: Blue cheese–stuffed olive, mezcal mist, Marcona almonds

- **2 oz. Gin Mare**
- **¼ oz. Dolin Blanc Vermouth**
- **¼ oz. manzanilla sherry**
- **¼ oz. Nardini Mandorla**
- **¼ oz. Del Maguey Ibérico Mezcal**
- **Barspoon Licor 43**
- **2 dashes Saline Solution (see recipe on page 14)**

1. Combine all of the ingredients in a bottle and put the bottle in the freezer.
2. To serve, pour the cocktail directly from the frozen bottle.
3. Garnish with a blue cheese–stuffed olive and spray the top of the drink with mezcal mist. Serve with a small ramekin of Marcona almonds.

COCONUT SAZERAC

SWEET LIBERTY DRINKS & SUPPLY COMPANY
237 20TH STREET SUITE B, MIAMI BEACH

A close relative to the Old Fashioned, the classic Sazerac has similar ingredients—rye whiskey takes the place of bourbon, Peychaud's bitters replaces Angostura bitters, and absinthe enters the recipe. Born around the mid-nineteenth century in New Orleans, the original Sazerac was crafted with cognac. The name comes from a popular brand of cognac imported to New Orleans, Sazerac de Forge & Fils, but a wine blight in 1870 created a shortage, and American rye whiskey then took the lead. Creative director Naren Young loves this cocktail for its fat-washed coconut oil that lends a "beautiful, oily, unctuous, buttery kind of texture. Coconut is so pervasive in tropical, sunny climates like Florida, and people come in wanting Piña Coladas and coconut-forward drinks. This is something different that balances a serious cocktail with Miami fun," he says. The fat-wash leaves a clear, unctuous texture that Young loves. To make coconut smoke, use dry coconut husks in your cocktail-smoking setup.

GLASSWARE: Etched rocks glass
GARNISH: Absinthe mist, coconut smoke

- 1¼ oz. Russell's Whiskey Reserve 6 Year Old Rye
- 1¼ oz. Pierre Ferrand 1840 Original Formula Cognac
- Coconut Fat Wash (see recipe), to taste
- 5 dashes Peychaud's bitters
- ¼ oz. Kalani Coconut Liqueur
- ¼ oz. Giffard Coconut Syrup

1. In a container, combine the whiskey, cognac, Coconut Fat Wash, and bitters and place the container in the freezer overnight.

2. Skim the fat layer off the top of the mixture and fine-strain the liquid into a rocks glass.

3. Add the coconut liqueur and coconut syrup, layering the tropical flavors.

4. To garnish, mist absinthe over the top of the cocktail, and spray coconut smoke into the glass to capture its aroma.

COCONUT FAT WASH: Toast coconut flakes, as needed, in a pan until they are brown. Add coconut oil, as needed, and melt it down, stirring. Remove from heat and allow the fat wash to cool.

THAT WATERMELON DRINK

SWEET LIBERTY DRINKS & SUPPLY COMPANY
237 20TH STREET SUITE B, MIAMI BEACH

Naren Young loves this cheeky riff on a Margarita. "I wanted to create something with watermelon and cilantro because the flavors work really well together. After workshopping some, we hit on this. There's some spice in there. There's some savoriness; there's a touch of bitterness from the aperitivo. You get a hint of smoke but not too much. It's just super fresh and crushable," he says.

GLASSWARE: Rocks glass
GARNISH: Cilantro sprig

- Tajín, for the rim
- 1 oz. El Tequileño Blanco Tequila
- ¾ oz. watermelon juice
- ½ oz. fresh lemon juice
- ½ oz. spicy agave nectar
- ½ oz. Montelobos Mezcal Espadín
- ¼ oz. Select Aperitivo
- 5 drops white balsamic vinegar
- 2 sprigs of cilantro
- 4 cucumber wheels

1. Wet half the rim of a rocks glass then dip the glass in Tajín.
2. Combine the remaining ingredients in a cocktail shaker with ice and shake.
3. Fine-strain the cocktail over ice into a rocks glass.
4. Garnish with a sprig of cilantro.

REMEMBERING JOHN LERMAYER

The Florida cocktail scene likely wouldn't have evolved into the experimental playground it is today if award-winning New York bartender and legendary drinks master John Lermayer had not moved to Miami in 2004. There he worked at SkyBar at Shore Club. The cocktail guru would go on to pour drinks at the White House, drink sherry in a Spanish distiller's private gallery "filled with hundreds of Picassos," as he said, and wring every moment out of life.

Lermayer focused on fresh ingredients, classic cocktails, and the art of hospitality. In 2007, Lenny Kravitz and Ben Pundhole tapped him to create cocktails for the Florida Room, which became a training ground for many award-winning bartenders. He brought in top cocktail educators and bartenders from around the globe to escalate Miami's cocktail scene. In 2012, John joined forces with Julio Cabrera at The Regent Cocktail Club to bring Prohibition era–style cocktails to the forefront in Miami. In 2016, he launched Sweet Liberty with Dan Binkiewicz and restaurateurs David Martinez and Michelle Bernstein. One year later, it won Best New American Bar at Tales of the Cocktail Foundation Spirited Awards and landed at number 27 in the World's 50 Best Bars.

Lermay passed away in 2018, but his influence on the entire cocktail industry remains. He was posthumously awarded the 2018 Helen David Lifetime Achievement Award at the Spirited Awards, and a grand parade of bartenders, owners, barbacks, writers, and people touched by his legacy traveled through the Marigny neighborhood of New Orleans, wearing John Lermayer shirts emblazoned with the words "He Will Always Be the Shit, Bro." So great was his impact in Miami that the city of Miami Beach declared June 21 John Lermayer Day.

KERN MATTEI JR., MAI-KAI

Tiki enthusiasts flocked to Mai-Kai, a fever dream of lagoons, lush tropical foliage, hula dancers, and fire-topped cocktails to partake in the escapism sweeping the United States in the 1950s. The Fort Lauderdale supper club, renowned for its immersive Polynesian experience has been listed on the National Register of Historic Places. The sprawling 26,000-square-foot space, inspired by Don the Beachcomber and Trader Vic's mid-century tiki palaces, houses one of Jeff "Beachbum" Berry's favorite bars, The Molokai Bar.

What started as two hundred seats has evolved into a six-hundred-seat establishment where they still serve the original recipes developed in 1956, like the Shark Bite and Black Magic. Kern Mattei Jr. carries on his father's legacy as the Mai-Kai's general manager. "People loved this place when it opened," Mattei Jr. says. "They went out for dinner in suits and mink coats, and it was the only place like it in Florida."

Kern Mattei Jr. started barbacking there in 1984, while he was still in high school. His father, Kern Mattei Sr., managed the restaurant from 1963 until 1991, and his mother was a Mai-Kai dancer.

In October 2020, a roof collapse led to Mai-Kai's first extended closure in its more-than-sixty-year history. The overwhelming scope and cost of the restoration kept the establishment shuttered until 2024, when Bill Fuller stepped in to save the historic venue and modernize its

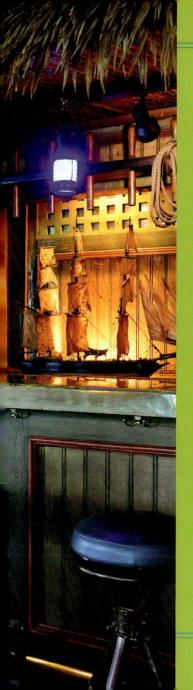

bones so future generations can experience tiki culture as those before them have.

"I've been creating cocktails here for years," Kern Mattei Jr. says. "Some of the old-time bartenders took me under their wings and showed me how you hold the bar bottle when you make a drink, and then how to make it, and to always make sure you taste it. I've been here for thirty years, like my dad before me, and I want every drink at the Mai-Kai to taste the same as it might have fifty years ago. When adding new drinks, I keep the old flare so it tastes like a vintage cocktail—but maybe with a hint of lemongrass or mezcal for a smoky flavor or a spicy pepper for some heat. We have new flavors, new products, and interesting tinctures, adding a modern twist while honoring the historic perspective on the drink."

MARA-AMU

MAI KAI
3599 NORTH FEDERAL HIGHWAY, FORT LAUDERDALE

Tahitian for "when the west wind blows," the Mara-Amu is one of the most popular tropical drinks on the Mai-Kai drinks menu. It's the only one that comes in a Mai-Kai tiki mug you can take home and is filled with fresh Florida juices.

GLASSWARE: Tiki mug

- ¾ oz. Bacardí Superior White Rum
- ¾ oz. Appleton Estate Signature Jamaica Rum
- ¾ oz. fresh orange juice
- ¾ oz. fresh grapefruit juice
- ¾ oz. passion fruit syrup
- ½ oz. fresh lime juice

1. Combine all of the ingredients in a cocktail shaker with ice and shake vigorously for 5 to 10 seconds, or mix for 3 to 5 seconds in a flash blender.

2. Strain the cocktail over ice cubes into your favorite tiki mug and serve with a straw.

DERBY DAIQUIRI

MAI KAI

3599 NORTH FEDERAL HIGHWAY, FORT LAUDERDALE

Created in 1959, when the organizers of the Florida Derby were looking for a drink of their own to compete with the Kentucky Derby's Mint Julep, the Derby Daiquiri became the race's official drink. It's a light and refreshing cocktail that is perfect for a Florida afternoon.

GLASSWARE: Small wine goblet

- ½ oz. fresh lime juice
- ½ oz. Simple Syrup (see recipe on page 14)
- 1 oz. fresh orange juice
- 1½ oz. Bacardí Superior White Rum

1. Place all of the ingredients in a blender with 1 cup of crushed ice and blend until smooth.

2. Serve in a small wine goblet or other stemmed glass with a straw and enjoy.

SAMANTHA NIEVES-RIVERA, BALL & CHAIN SALOON

The best Mojito in Miami belongs to Ball & Chain, and it has been on the menu since day one. "Out in the sun, in the Florida heat, you are ready for that cocktail with all its fresh ingredients, filled with crushed ice—it's extremely refreshing," says Samantha Nieves-Rivera, beverage and events manager.

Ball & Chain Saloon opened in 1935 and remained open into the 1950s with some slight name alterations. Popular performers like Billie Holiday, Count Basie, and Chet Baker played there. When a large influx of Cubans fleeing dictatorial rule arrived, the area became

known as Little Havana. Ball & Chain went through other incarnations and even stood vacant for twenty years, until Mad Room Hospitality began an extensive renovation and prepared to reopen the storied neighborhood restaurant and bar.

Nieves-Rivera grew up in Puerto Rico, where she bartended for almost ten years before moving to New York. She arrived in Miami via a job with Carnival Cruise Line. She keeps the focus of her cocktail program on Cuban history. "Bartending and the art of crafting cocktails are well respected in Cuba. We wanted to honor that cantinero lifestyle," she says. Stop in for the Mojito, and stay for the live salsa and jazz music.

THE WORLD-FAMOUS MOJITO

BALL & CHAIN SALOON
1513 SOUTHWEST 8TH STREET, MIAMI

This award-winning Mojito embraces the classic recipe that originated at La Bodeguita del Medio in Cuba. Before you add your mint sprig garnish, give it a slap in your hand to release the essential oils and amplify the flavor and aroma. Samantha Nieves-Rivera, beverage and events manager, uses yerba buena and advises that, when muddling, you be sure to not butcher the leaves.

GLASSWARE: Highball glass

GLASSWARE: Mint sprig, sugarcane stalk

- **6 yerba buena mint leaves**
- **½ oz. fresh lime juice**
- **1½ oz. Bacardí Superior White Rum**
- **¾ oz. Simple Syrup (see recipe on page 14)**
- **1 teaspoon sugar**
- **Soda water, to top**

1. In a highball glass, slightly muddle the mint leaves along with the lime juice.

2. Add the remaining ingredients, except for the soda, then fill the glass with crushed ice.

3. Stir the mixture thoroughly and top with soda water.

4. Garnish with a mint sprig and sugarcane.

DEMERARA SIMPLE SYRUP: In a saucepan over medium-low heat, combine 1 cup demerara sugar and 1 cup water and simmer, stirring until the sugar is dissolved. Allow the syrup to cool. (To make rich demerara simple syrup, double the amount of sugar.)

BALL & CHAIN

CALLE OCHO OLD FASHIONED

BALL & CHAIN SALOON
1513 SOUTHWEST 8TH STREET, MIAMI

Samantha Nieves-Rivera wanted to make something inspired by Cuba but not your typical Cuban cocktail, and so the Calle Ocho Old Fashioned was born. "We infused our Angostura bitters with fresh tobacco leaves," she says. "We have the luck of having cigar shops right next door and are very close with our neighbors, so we get our fresh tobacco from them and add it to our Angostura for a Cuba-inspired Old Fashioned."

GLASSWARE: Rocks glass

GARNISH: Dry tobacco leaf

- **2 oz. Bacardí Reserva Ocho**
- **¼ oz. Demerara Simple Syrup (see recipe)**
- **3 dashes tobacco bitters**

1. Combine all of the ingredients in a mixing glass with ice cubes and stir for 8 seconds.
2. Strain the cocktail over fresh ice into a rocks glass.
3. Garnish with a dry tobacco leaf.

PASTELITO DAIQUIRI

BALL & CHAIN SALOON
1513 SOUTHWEST 8TH STREET, MIAMI

On the menu since day one, the Pastelito Daquiri, according to Samantha Nieves-Rivera, is "two treats in one." The cocktail follows the classic Daquiri tenets of sugar and rum but diverts with the inclusion of pureed, fresh Florida guava. The whimsical garnish, a pastelito, adds another layer of Cuban culture to Ball & Chain's cocktail program—the guava-filled puff pastry is a traditional sweet served in households around Cuba and Little Havana in Miami.

GLASSWARE: Coupe glass

GARNISH: Skewered pastelito

- 1½ oz. Bacardí Superior White Rum
- ¾ oz. fresh lime juice
- ¾ oz. guava puree
- ½ oz. Simple Syrup (see recipe on page 14)

1. Chill a coupe glass. Combine all of the ingredients in a cocktail shaker with ice and shake vigorously.
2. Strain the cocktail into the chilled coupe.
3. Garnish with a skewered pastelito.

GUAVA SANGRIA

BALL & CHAIN SALOON
1513 SOUTHWEST 8TH STREET, MIAMI

For the Cuban version of the popular Spanish beverage, Sangria, Samantha Riviera-Nieves adds ingredients popular in the Cuban community: guava puree, Cuban rum, and amaretto transport you to a hot night in Havana where the congas are beating out a rhythm. This recipe calls for orange, mint, and mixed fruits to macerate in the glass, but grab whatever is fresh at the market you love. You can also make batches of this Sangria by multiplying the recipe by number of servings desired.

GLASSWARE: Hurricane glass

GARNISH: Orange slice, mint sprig

- 2 oz. pineapple juice
- 2 oz. guava puree
- 1½ oz. Havana Club Añejo 3 Años
- 1 oz. amaretto liqueur
- 1 oz. fresh lime juice
- ½ oz. pinot noir, to top

1. Combine all of the ingredients, except for the wine, in a cocktail shaker with ice and shake well.
2. Fill a hurricane glass with crushed ice and strain the cocktail into the glass. Top with the wine.
3. Garnish with fruits and mint.

JULIO AND ANDY CABRERA, CAFÉ LA TROVA

At Café La Trova, where the congas set the tempo for the dance floor, the show is behind the bar. That's where the cantineros, professional Cuban bartenders, create music of their own with their shakers. Julio Cabrera, award-winning master cantinero and co-owner of Café La Trova, brings the proud Cuban tradition of professional bartending to the Miami community every night through his menu of classic cocktails, his mentoring of fledgling bartenders, and the La Trova style of music played by their Grammy Award–winning band.

In 1998, Cabrera and a group of bartenders resurrected the Club de Cantineros, a Cuba-based professional association for bartenders that ran from the 1920s until the 1950s, as the Association of Cuban Cantineros. Cabrera threw a party at Café La Trova to celebrate the guild's hundredth anniversary. "It's a profession for life, and like any profession, you have to go to school just like doctors, lawyers, and dentists," he says.

Not just any bartender can be a cantinero. First, you must know more than two hundred classic cocktail recipes. Then there's the uniform—bartending jackets, black leather shoes, sleeves down to your wrists. But mostly you need to be a master of hospitality. "If you work behind the bar, you move with the music, dance with the customer. We are Cuban, and in Cuba live music is in every bar, in every place you work, part of every day. I wanted to bring that authentic Cuban culture to Miami," Cabrera says.

DAIQUIRÍ CLÁSICO

CAFÉ LA TROVA
971 SOUTHWEST 8TH STREET, MIAMI

When Julio Cabrera started his cantinero journey thirty-five years ago, the Daiquirí Clásico was one of the first drinks he had to master. When he arrived in the United States twenty years ago, all he found were frozen strawberry and mango Daiquiris from machines. Bacardí hired Cabrera to be a Daiquiri ambassador and tour the United States teaching people how to make the Daiquirí Clásico. "I brought bartenders from the United States to Santiago, Cuba, twice a year, the place where Daiquiris were first made," he said. The 1896 classic version is credited to Jennings Cox, an American engineer who lived and worked in Cuba after the Spanish-American War, after he ran out of gin at a cocktail party. He used rum, and the Daiquiri was born. The frozen version came out in 1927, when the first blender was delivered to the Floridita bar in Havana. Though Cabrera used Bacardí in his early Daiquiris, any good quality white rum will do.

GLASSWARE: Coupe glass

GARNISH: Freshly grated nutmeg, mint sprig, pineapple wedge

- ½ tablespoon white granulated sugar
- ¾ oz. fresh lime juice
- 2 oz. white rum

1. Combine the sugar and lime juice in a cocktail shaker and stir until the sugar is dissolved.
2. Add the rum and ice and shake vigorously.
3. Strain the cocktail into a coupe.
4. Garnish with freshly grated nutmeg, a mint sprig, and a pineapple wedge.

FLAMINGO MOJITO

CAFÉ LA TROVA
971 SOUTHWEST 8TH STREET, MIAMI

A little pink always makes a Mojito more fun, and it's even better if that color comes from watermelon juice. Julio Cabrera developed this tongue-in-cheek version of the classic Cuban cocktail to pay homage to the most iconic of Florida's birds, the pink flamingo. "The ginger and the watermelon make this so refreshing and tropical but also so Florida," Cabrera said.

GLASSWARE: Collins glass

GARNISH: Fresh mint sprig, 2 watermelon cubes on a skewer

- **2 oz. white rum**
- **2 oz. fresh watermelon juice**
- **¾ oz. Ginger Syrup (see recipe)**
- **¾ oz. fresh lime juice**
- **6 to 8 mint leaves**
- **Club soda, to top**

1. Combine all of the ingredients, except for the club soda, in a cocktail shaker with ice and shake.
2. Double-strain the cocktail into a collins glass with ice.
3. Top with club soda and garnish with a mint sprig and 2 watermelon cubes on a skewer.

GINGER SYRUP: Combine 14 oz. Simple Syrup (see recipe on page 14) and 2 oz. fresh ginger juice and stir well.

TROVA SWIZZLE

971 SOUTHWEST 8TH STREET, MIAMI

Cantinero Andy Cabrera developed this take on the classic Swizzle cocktail that takes the original recipe a step further with the addition of the pineapple shrub. The apple cider vinegar adds an element of sourness to the cocktail known as the national drink of Bermuda.

GLASSWARE: Hurricane glass

GARNISH: Pineapple slice sprinkled with Tajín

- 2 oz. Clément VSOP Rhum Vieux
- 1 oz. Pineapple Shrub (see recipe)
- ½ oz. Rich Demerara Simple Syrup (see recipe on page 44)
- ¼ oz. fresh lime juice

1. Combine all of the ingredients in a highball glass over crushed ice.

2. Top with club soda.

3. Garnish with a pineapple slice sprinkled with Tajín.

PINEAPPLE SHRUB: Combine 500 grams granulated sugar and 500 grams canned pineapple juice and mix until the sugar is dissolved. Then add 500 grams apple cider vinegar and finish mixing.

TOASTED COCONUT SYRUP: In a blender, combine 8 oz. Semi-Rich Simple Syrup (see recipe on page 14) and 8 grams toasted coconut flakes and blend on high for 1 minute. Strain the syrup through a cheese-cloth. Reserve the coconut flakes for the Coquito Snack.

COQUITO SNACK: Using the leftover coconut flakes covered in syrup from the Toasted Coconut Syrup, mold them into a circle and, in the oven, dehydrate the circle at 150°F for 12 hours. Add orange food coloring, as needed, to make the color pop.

CUMBANCHERO

Designed around the sensibilities of 1970s Miami's Cuban scene, La Cumbancha, now closed, had professional bartenders trained by Julio and Andy Cabrera, Latin food from all over, and a dance-worthy international playlist. The cocktail program was inspired by Andy Cabrera's travels around the world with his father.

GLASSWARE: Tiki glass

GARNISH: Fresh mint sprig, Coquito Snack (see recipe)

- 2 oz. Rum Blend (see recipe)
- 1¼ oz. pineapple juice
- ¾ oz. fresh lime juice
- ½ oz. Campari
- ½ oz. Toasted Coconut Syrup (see recipe)

1. Combine all of the ingredients in a cocktail shaker with ice and shake.

2. Strain the cocktail into a tiki glass with crushed ice.

3. Garnish with a fresh mint sprig and coquito snack.

RUM BLEND: In a small glass container, create a mixture that is 1 oz. (30 ml) añejo rum, ⅔ oz. (20 ml) spiced rum, and 2½ teaspoons (12 ml) overproof rum. If you want to upsize your batch, the ratio is 50% añejo, 30% spiced, and 20% overproof rum.

JOSEPH LLONTOP, BELLA BELLA AND BAR 1903

Bar 1903 manager Joseph Llontop came to Tallahassee to go to Florida State University and never left. After graduating, he stuck around doing photography. When some friends opened Liberty Bar, he signed on to be part of the opening staff. Joseph got sucked in and fell in love with the cocktail industry. "Liberty Bar had one of the first true craft cocktail programs in Tallahassee," Llontop says. "They dove into having fresh ingredients from the farm and focused on spirit education, and I got thrown into something I didn't know I had such a passion for."

Ten years later, he splits his time managing Italian restaurant Bella Bella and Bar 1903. Though he has put in his time working at late-night bars, fine dining, and gig work at weddings, concerts, and bartending in general, the craft side of the industry has always captured his imagination. "The quality, attention to detail, and making a cocktail into a piece of art satisfies the artist in me."

The historically designated building housing Bar 1903 was one of Florida's first libraries. The bar has a speakeasy atmosphere with an intimate thirty-five seats and its first-come, first-serve approach.

Storytelling drives much of the house beverage menu. During research and development, Llontop prods his bartenders to share their vision for drinks—the flavor profile, how they see it—and then, in true artist fashion, they draw it out and figure out the ingredients. "I'm always looking for a childhood story or some narrative moment in their lives," he says. A story about a grandmother and strawberry candies became a drink that brought back those memories. A legendary lemon bar recipe from another bartender's grandmother became a Lemon Bar Martini that captured the tang of the curd and the buttery shortbread of the dessert.

But a lot of cocktails in Florida are geared toward that escapist feeling that dominated the state's tiki cocktail culture in the 1950s and beyond. "I want a drink that transports me to that tropical paradise for a moment," Llontop says, "that provides that sense of relief, where you can just exhale and focus on your drink, and everything else goes away. It makes me want to be back on the river, by the beach, in a sinkhole, just floating somewhere with a good drink."

FREE WILLY STRIKES BACK

BAR 1903
209 EAST PARK AVENUE, TALLAHASSEE

Bar 1903 manager Joseph Llontop holds nostalgic love for the movie *Free Willy*, which inspired this drink. "It's got umami flavors, a little bit of salinity, tropical notes from the coconut and lychee, and then the honeydew foam lingers throughout the entire drink," Llontop says. "This blue cocktail with subtle seafoam green on top—it's a drink that immediately gets photographed for the 'gram."

GLASSWARE: Nick & Nora glass

GARNISH: Honeydew Foam (see recipe)

- 1½ oz. Seaweed & Kelp–Infused Grey Whale Gin (see recipe)
- 1½ oz. Lychee & Blue Spirulina Syrup (see recipe)
- ½ oz. Luxardo Bitter Bianco
- ½ oz. fresh lime juice
- ¼ oz. Coco López Cream of Coconut

1. Combine all of the ingredients in a cocktail shaker with chip ice and shake.

2. Double-strain the cocktail into a Nick & Nora.

3. To garnish, rope with Honeydew Foam from an iSi whipped cream canister.

SEAWEED & KELP–INFUSED GRAY WHALE GIN: Blanch seaweed and kelp in hot water for 1 minute or less to activate it. You can then go about the infusion in two different ways. If you don't have an iSi whipped cream canister, pour 1 (750 ml) bottle of gin over the sea-weed and kelp and let the infusion sit overnight, then strain. If you have an iSi whipped cream canister, you can do a rapid infusion: Put small pieces of seaweed and kelp, along with the gin, to fill the canister half-way. Charge it twice with N2O and shake vigorously, then let it rest for 5 minutes. The resulting gin should take on the hints of salinity and umami of the kelp.

LYCHEE & BLUE SPIRULINA SYRUP: Pour a can of lychees along with the syrup they come in into a saucepan over low heat. Mash the lychees and add white sugar, to taste, then reduce the syrup to your de-sired thickness. Strain out any large particulates and throw the syrup in the blender with 1 tablespoon organic blue spirulina powder and blend to incorporate.

HONEYDEW FOAM: Deseed and cut away the skin of 1 ripe honey-dew melon, then throw the melon in a blender with some water and blend until smooth. Fine-strain out the pulp and return the juice to the blender. Add white sugar, to taste, and blend to create a light syrup, then add a dash lemon juice for acidity and a few drops of Saline Solution (see recipe on page 14) and blend. Add 2 teaspoons xan-thum gum to thicken the syrup, which helps create a thick yet silky foam that will linger the whole time you're drinking your cocktail. Add the foam to an iSi canister and double charge. Keep the can-ister cool.

PASTELITO PAPI

BAR 1903
209 EAST PARK AVENUE, TALLAHASSEE

Joseph Llontop hails from Westin, a town located between Fort Lauderdale and Miami, but his roots are Peruvian. "I grew up in a very Latino household and I remember eating pastelitos, the buttery puff pastry wrapped around guava and cream cheese, on hot summer days," he says. He took that nostalgic childhood memory and transformed it into a cocktail with a brown butter fat–washed rum to mimic the puff pastry, and a guava syrup to bring in that tropical fruit flavor. But he couldn't leave out the cream cheese so he created a whipped cream with cream cheese as the base. "Everyone drinks with their eyes first so I put the cocktail in this chubby little glass and spiral the cream cheese whip up like soft serve," he says.

GLASSWARE: Snifter glass

GARNISH: Cream Cheese Whip (see recipe),
mint bouquet, lemon zest

- 1½ oz. Brown Butter Fat-Washed Rum Blend (see recipe)
- 2 oz. Guava Syrup (see recipe)
- ½ oz. Punt e Mes
- ½ oz. Carpano Bianco
- ½ oz. fresh lemon juice
- 2 dashes Angostura bitters

1. Combine all of the ingredients in a cocktail shaker with chip ice and shake.

2. Pour the cocktail into a snifter and top with pebble ice.

3. To garnish, spiral up the Cream Cheese Whip and add a mint bouquet and freshly grated lemon zest.

BROWN BUTTER FAT-WASHED RUM BLEND: In a pan over low heat, cook butter, to taste, until it is melted and browned. In a container, combine equal parts Bacardí Superior White Rum and Angostura 7-Year-Old Rum. Add the butter, store the mixture in the freezer overnight, and then strain the rum blend through a cheesecloth or coffee filter. Rebottle.

GUAVA SYRUP: Empty a full jar of Conchita Guava Preserves into a saucepan over low heat and heat the preserves to soften them. Using the same jar, fill it with water and pour the water into the pot. As the mixture begins to dissolve and combine, use the same jar again, filling it with turbinado sugar, and add the sugar to the mixture, stirring until the sugar is dissolved.

CREAM CHEESE WHIP: Soften a block of cream cheese, then combine the cream cheese with 2 cups heavy whipping cream, ½ cup sifted powdered sugar, and 1 teaspoon vanilla extract. Whip until the mixture is well incorporated. Load the mixture into an iSi canister and charge twice with N_2O cream charger.

THE CHARTREUSE CRISIS

In the eighteenth century, Carthusian monks in the Chartreuse Mountains in France began crafting Chartreuse based on a secret recipe created by a medieval alchemist in 1605 for an "elixir for long life." The recipe calls for one hundred and thirty different herbs, plants, and flowers, and today only three monks know the full recipe. The monks remain the sole producers of the spirit, and in 2023 they announced their decision to "protect their monastic life and devote their time to solitude and prayer" by capping production at roughly 1.2 million bottles a year. This is not fewer bottles, but as home bars sprung up throughout the pandemic, demand for it increased exponentially. Both the green and yellow versions of Chartreuse, with their aromatic, bold, herbal flavor, have inspired legions of bartenders to create signature cocktails dependent on the spirit. Harry Johnson created the Bijou in the 1890s, in 1915 Frank Fogarty invented The Last Word, Joaquín Símo created the Naked & Famous in 2011, and that same year Ted Kilgore developed the Industry Sour in St Louis. Though the flavors differ slightly from barrel to barrel, the original Green Chartreuse delivers earthy, herbal, peppery, and zesty notes while its yellow counterpart offers a rounder, more honeyed flavor.

If a cocktail with Chartreuse is on the agenda and there is none on the shelves, a few substitutes have emerged. Dolin Génépy, an alpine herbal liqueur, has a lower ABV and slightly subtler flavor. Faccia Brutto's Centerbe is "an Italian take on Chartreuse, translating to 'one hundred herbs.'" Ver By Elixir Craft Spirits, Chaparral by Brucato Amaro, and BroVo Spirits' Uncharted Rhapsody American Forest Liqueur all will do in a pinch.

JOHN MOORE, FORGOTTEN TONIC

John Moore hated his job in electrical engineering, so he took a busboy position at P.F. Chang's. He fell in love with the hospitality industry. On his days off, he organized the spirits room to learn what each bottle looked like for his evenings as a barback.

Enter Todd Lineberry, who had just opened a couple of barbecue restaurants. He asked Moore to come and head up his whiskey program. That conversation evolved into a friendship that saw Moore go on to set up bar programs and open new locations for Mojo BBQ.

On January 1, 2019, Moore struck out on his own and took over what would become Forgotten Tonic on Aviles Street, the oldest street in the United States, in the nation's oldest city—St. Augustine. The plot of land it sat on had once been home to a Spanish hospital and was also where the home of Don Pedro Menéndez de Avilés, founder of St. Augustine, once stood. Because of the age of the property, Moore had to involve the city archeologist as he worked to renovate the space.

As for the name, "Bars and restaurants are like remedies, places where people go to celebrate or to escape," he says. "And isn't a tonic a remedy? Being the oldest street in the country is important, but it often gets forgotten amid the forts and the bridges and St. George Street. The connotation of these two words put together made sense for this building, this restaurant, this area of the city."

Forgotten Tonic boasts an eclectic food menu of dishes like Bibimbap, Pasta Alla Vodka, and Shrimp & Grits Étouffée alongside an encyclopedic cocktail program that serves as a training ground for promising bartenders. "I am here today because of a guy that sat across from the dishwasher at the bar. I was friendly with him, and he was friendly. And it blossomed into a fulfilling career I had no idea I would love so much.

FORGOTTEN TONIC

FORGOTTEN TONIC
6 AVILES STREET, ST. AUGUSTINE

Venue owner John Moore wanted a Spanish-style Gin & Tonic with different botanical notes for his namesake cocktail. "It tastes like gin on steroids. It's this minty, refreshing, delicious cocktail," he says.

GLASSWARE: Wineglass

GARNISH: Lime wheel, cucumber ribbon, star anise pod, mint bouquet

- 4½ oz. sparkling mineral water
- ¾ oz. Tonic Syrup (see recipe)
- ¾ oz. BroVo Uncharted Rhapsody American Forest Liqueur
- ¾ oz. Lime Oil–Infused Navy Strength Gin (see recipe)
- ½ oz. Dolin Génépy le Chamois Liqueur

1. Combine all of the ingredients in a stemmed wineglass and stir to combine.
2. Add cubed ice and garnish with a lime wheel, cucumber ribbon, mint bouquet, and star anise pod. Finish it off with a straw.

TONIC SYRUP: Zest 1 lemon, 1 lime, and ½ orange. Chop 1 small lemongrass stalk. Crack ½ teaspoon allspice berries, ½ teaspoon coriander seeds, and ½ teaspoon cardamom pods and toast for 1 to 2 minutes, until they become fragrant and slightly darker in color. In a medium saucepan, combine the citrus zests, chopped lemongrass, toasted spices, and 1 oz. finely ground cinchona bark with 2 cups water. Bring the mixture to a boil, then reduce the heat to low and let it simmer for 30 minutes. Remove the saucepan from heat and let the mixture cool. Strain it through a nut milk bag into a clean container to remove the solids. Press down on the solids to extract as much liquid as possible. Pour the mixture into a clean saucepan over medium low heat and add 1 cup cane sugar, 2 tablespoons citric acid, ⅛ teaspoon salt, ¼ teaspoon vanilla extract, and ½ teaspoon lavender buds and simmer, stirring until the sugar, salt, and powders are dissolved. Let the syrup cool and strain. Store it in the refrigerator and use within 2 weeks.

LIME OIL–INFUSED NAVY STRENGTH GIN: In a sealable glass container, combine 1 (750 ml) bottle of Hayman's Royal Dock Gin, 52 grams lime zest, 25 grams malic acid, and 0.2 grams ascorbic acid and stir. Seal the container and let the mixture sit for 25 minutes. Strain the infused gin through a coffee filter and store it in a cool, dark place.

ESCAPE FROM BLACK MOUNTAIN

FORGOTTEN TONIC
6 AVILES STREET, ST. AUGUSTINE

For this play on a Painkiller, venue owner John Moore wanted to balance the sweetness of the original recipes with overproof rum and lime juice. It won the 2017 Florida Montenegro competition. "Even though it is a pretty basic structure, this cocktail tastes really good," Moore says.

GLASSWARE: Hurricane glass

GARNISH: Orange wheel, lime wheel, mint bouquet, grated nutmeg

- 1½ oz. Amaro Montenegro
- 1½ oz. orange juice
- 1½ oz. Coconut Cream (see recipe)
- ½ oz. Planteray O.F.T.D. Overproof Rum
- ½ oz. fresh lime juice
- Dash Angostura bitters

1. Combine all of the ingredients in a cocktail shaker with pebble ice a shake a few times to mix the ingredients.
2. Pour the cocktail into a hurricane glass.
3. Add extra pebble ice as needed before garnishing with an orange wheel, lime wheel, mint bouquet, and freshly grated nutmeg.

COCONUT CREAM: Crack 1 gram star anise and 1 gram whole cloves. In a pan, toast the spices until they are aromatic. In a bowl, combine 400 grams sugar, 4 grams kosher salt, and 0.8 gram xanthan gum and stir to evenly distribute. Combine the toasted spices, the sugar mixture, 250 grams filtered water, and 600 grams coconut milk in a large pot over medium heat. Add 2 grams lime zest and 1.5 grams orange zest and stir until the sugar is dissolved. Bring the mixture to a low boil then immediately turn off the heat. Let the cream steep for 30 minutes. Filter it through a fine-mesh strainer and store in the refrigerator.

I CAN'T EVEN

FORGOTTEN TONIC
6 AVILES STREET, ST. AUGUSTINE

Mezcal is so artisanal, so rooted in the little town that it comes from," venue owner John Moore says. To quench the thirst for Mezcal cocktails, he developed this adventurous cocktail that employs Florida's fresh strawberries, grapefruit, and lime.

GLASSWARE: Double rocks glass
GARNISH: Cucumber ribbon

- 1½ oz. blanco tequila
- ¾ oz. Strawberry-Jalapeño Shrub (see recipe)
- ¾ oz. grapefruit juice
- ½ oz. Aperol
- ½ oz. fresh lime juice
- ¼ oz. joven mezcal

1. Combine all of the ingredients in a cocktail shaker with ice and shake.
2. Double-strain the cocktail into double rocks glass over a large ice cube.
3. Garnish with a cucumber ribbon.

STRAWBERRY-JALAPEÑO SHRUB: Combine 250 grams strawberries, hulled; 250 grams sugar; 50 grams white wine vinegar; 1 gram star anise pod; and 24 grams chopped jalapeño in a container. Cover the container and let the mixture sit for 7 days, mixing daily. Fine-strain the shrub using an apple press and nut milk bag. Store it in the refrigerator.

RAISING CANE

FORGOTTEN TONIC
6 AVILES STREET, ST. AUGUSTINE

The first modern cocktail John Moore put on his menu was the Raising Cane. "It's not super boozy. It's a light and refreshing cocktail for a hot day sitting on the patio," he says.

GLASSWARE: Coupe glass

GARNISH: Mint leaf, lemon wheel

- 1½ oz. vodka
- ¾ oz. Blackberry Lemongrass Shrub (see recipe)
- ½ oz. Thatcher's Elderflower Liqueur
- ½ oz. fresh lemon juice
- ¼ oz. rich (2:1) honey syrup
- Lemon twist, to express

1. Chill a coupe glass. Combine all of the ingredients, except for the lemon twist, in a cocktail shaker with ice and shake.
2. Strain the cocktail into the chilled coupe.
3. Express the lemon twist over the cocktail and discard.
4. Garnish with a mint leaf and a lemon wheel.

BLACKBERRY LEMONGRASS SHRUB: In a container, combine 250 grams blackberries, 250 grams granulated sugar, 50 grams white wine vinegar, and 24 grams chopped lemongrass and stir to combine. Cover and let the mixture sit for 7 days, mixing daily. Fine-strain the shrub using an apple press and nut milk bag. Store it in the refrigerator.

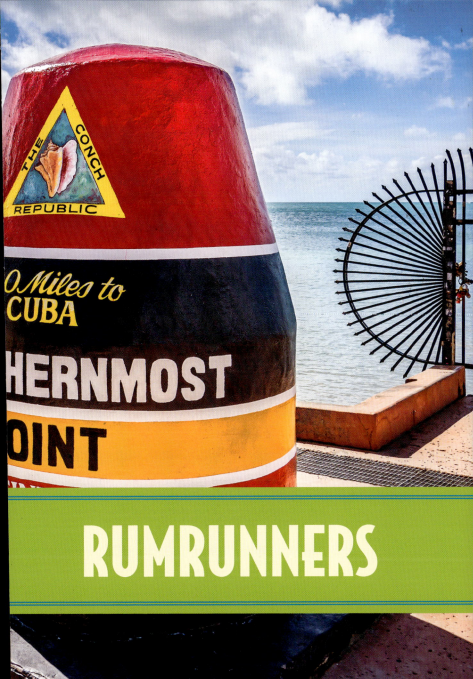

RUMRUNNERS

During Prohibition, Florida's notorious rumrunners illegally transported rum from the Caribbean into the United States. One of the most legendary, "Captain" Bill McCoy, inspired the phrase "The Real McCoy" because he never diluted or altered his alcohol—buyers always got the pure spirits.

McCoy smuggled between Bimini and the Bahamas to South Florida, running the "Rum Line," as it became known, to transport vessels awaiting in "Rum Row," an area of international waters off the coast.

National Prohibition took effect in January 1920. In the three and a half years that followed, before his capture and arrest, McCoy and other rumrunners used false floors and secret cargo holds to do the work of transporting Caribbean liquor to the States. According to Jena Ellenwood, who grew up across the Halifax River from the house McCoy once lived in, McCoy "had [bottles] stacked, not in cases, but he would make a little pyramid, sew it up in burlap, and they were called 'hams.'"

RUM RUNNER

Opened in 1969, the original Holiday Isle Tiki Bar transported guests to a tropical paradise with its bamboo furniture, Polynesian masks, dim lighting, beach views, and tiki cocktails. John Ebert concocted the Rum Runner, their signature drink, as an homage to Florida's notorious rumrunners such as "Captain" Bill McCoy. Over the years, the Tiki Bar has evolved and changed flags but still embraces its nostalgic charm and signature drinks. "This classic cocktail captures the essence of our Tiki Bar with its balanced mix of rum, banana and blackberry liqueurs, and tropical juices. It's visually stunning and incredibly refreshing," says resort manager Hicham El Ibrik.

GLASSWARE: Rum Runner glass
GARNISH: Cherry, orange slice

- 2 oz. orange juice
- 1 oz. Don Q 151°
- 1 oz. fresh lime juice
- ¾ oz. Giffard Banane du Brésil
- ½ oz. grenadine
- ½ oz. Giffard Crème de Mûre

1. Combine all of the ingredients in a cocktail shaker with ice and shake.
2. Strain the cocktail into a Rum Runner glass filled with ice.
3. Garnish with an orange slice and a cherry.

CANE & BARREL PUNCH

CANE & BARREL ROOFTOP BAR
110 2ND STREET NORTH, ST. PETERSBURG

This is a single serving, but if you want to mix up a punch bowl to share with friends and family, multiply this recipe by eight and top with dehydrated citrus fruits, fresh orchids, and popping boba.

GLASSWARE: Double rocks glass

GARNISH: Mint, orange peel ribbon

- 1½ oz. rum
- 1½ oz. blood orange liqueur
- 1½ oz. Monin Honey Syrup
- ¾ oz. fresh lemon juice
- ¾ oz. orange juice
- ½ oz. Chinola Passion Fruit Liqueur
- Splash soda, to top

1. Combine all of the ingredients, except for the soda, in a cocktail shaker with crushed ice and shake.
2. Pour the cocktail into a double rocks glass and top with soda.
3. Garnish with fresh mint and an orange peel ribbon.

ACGT

This is AC Hotels' signature cocktail, crafted with gin and a house-made tonic and served in a custom glass to optimize aroma.

GLASSWARE: Highball glass

GARNISH: Lime wheel, orange swath

- 3 oz. club soda
- ½ oz. tonic water
- 1½ oz. Bombay Sapphire Gin

1. Combine all of the ingredients over ice in a highball and stir.

2. Garnish with a lime wheel and an orange swath.

CANE & SMOKE

Upscale cocktail lounges often serve smoked cocktails smoked under a large glass cloche and a tinderbox filled with aromatic wood chips—it's part of the spectacle. You can achieve that effect at home by getting your own cocktail smoker kit or by using a kitchen torch and cloche and sourcing cedar wood chips. The bar uses the Aged & Charred Smoke Top Cocktail Smoker Kit (which you can buy online).

GLASSWARE: Rocks glass

GARNISH: Cedar smoke, orange slice skewered with a maraschino cherry

- 1½ oz. **Ron Centenario 12 Gran Legado**
- 1½ oz. **Del Maguey Vida Clásico**
- ¾ oz. **Amaro Montenegro**
- ¼ oz. **Jack Rudy Cocktail Co. Demerara Syrup**
- 4 dashes **mole bitters**

1. Combine all of the ingredients in a cocktail shaker and stir.
2. Add a large ice cube to a rocks glass and pour the cocktail over top.
3. Top with cedar smoke, and garnish with an orange slice skewered with a maraschino cherry.

FRIDA'S FLOWERS

This take on a French 75 has a touch of pear, Cynar, and foaming bitters for complexity, cava for a touch of Spain, and edible flowers in honor of the drink's namesake, Frida Kahlo, who was known to weave flowers through her hair, wear vine-embroidered skirts, and paint birds of paradise, zinnia, irises, and more to "keep them from dying," as the Mexican artist said.

GLASSWARE: Nick & Nora glass

GARNISH: Edible flowers or dehydrated rose

- **1½ oz. Castle & Key Roots of Ruin Gin**
- **1½ oz. Cynar**
- **¾ oz. fresh lemon juice**
- **½ oz. Monin Desert Pear Syrup**
- **Splash cava**
- **4 dashes Ms. Better's Bitters Miraculous Foamer**

1. Combine all of the ingredients in a cocktail shaker with ice and shake.
2. Strain the cocktail into another shaker without ice and dry-shake.
3. Pour the cocktail into a Nick & Nora and garnish with edible flowers or dehydrated rose.

ROB CRABTREE AND WHITNEY HOBBS, BOAT DRINKS

Vintage paintings of boats and tropical fruit and sepia photographs depicting life on the water in bygone days decorate the walls at Boat Drinks in St. Augustine. Owners Rob Crabtree and Whitney Hobbs wanted to create a beachy bar with sought-after spirits—a wide selection of rum was a must—and syrups. Rob Crabtree worked in ocean engineering, taking a job in Miami that sent him all over the Caribbean designing marinas, cruise ports, and wave pools. He fell in love with Caribbean food and drinks and amassed a home rum collection from the islands. When the market crashed in the late aughts, Crabtree went all in on the hospitality industry. His home has been behind the bar for the past fifteen-plus years.

Whitney Hobbs worked at a tequila bar in Austin before becoming a brand ambassador for spirits marketing agency The Bon Vivants. "We threw crazy parties, went river rafting, and [arranged] anything that would create memorable experiences that bartenders would connect to the brands," Hobbs says.

After a short stint in Houston, Crabtree and Hobbs set sights on opening their own bar. "Boat drinks" alludes to a state of mind. "If you're on a boat or in your pool or by the water and you have a drink in your hand, you're having a good time," Crabtree says. "That's how it was for me growing up, and we wanted to replicate it here."

Near the end of 2019, Boat Drinks, the bar, set sail.

"I love Florida; it's in my blood," Crabtree says. "We saw the potential in St. Augustine. Nobody was doing good frozen or tropical drinks and all these historic Florida beach bars, dive bars, and marina bars were disappearing as development ramped up. I missed being on my dad's houseboat and hanging out in marina bars with him. I love that happy hour vibe, the camaraderie that erupts at four or five o'clock, when everyone decides it's time for drinks."

SCUTTLEBUTT SWIZZLE

BOAT DRINKS
56 ST GEORGE STREET, ST. AUGUSTINE

Co-owner Rob Crabtree advises that this take on a Jasper's Rum Punch recipe demands a rum that can stand up to bold flavors, so be sure to use an overproof Jamaican rum. Crabtree made a batch of the punch as Hurricane Michael blew into town in 2018, right before they opened the bar. "I knew it would keep my lime juice fresh and I had plenty of rum and ice so I made a couple quarts of it. We sipped it, adding a little soda water to dilute it slightly, and that version became the basis of the Scuttlebutt Swizzle," he says. They serve it filled with ice because the drink keeps evolving as it dilutes. "This is not for the faint of heart. She is beautiful. She's so delicious, and she's been on our menu since day one," co-owner Whitney Hobbs says.

GLASSWARE: Tall tropical glass

GARNISH: Freshly grated nutmeg, mint sprig

- 1½ oz. Hampden Estate Rum Fire
- 1½ oz. Scuttlebutt Mix (see recipe)
- Soda water, to top

1. Combine the rum and Scuttlebutt Mix in a cocktail shaker with a little ice and whip-shake.
2. Pour the cocktail into a tall tropical glass. Top with ice and soda water and swizzle to combine.
3. Garnish with freshly grated nutmeg and a mint sprig.

SCUTTLEBUTT MIX: Blend 2 oz. fresh lime juice and 2 oz. sugar in a blender until combined. Stir in 1 fat teaspoon Angostura bitters. Add in dried hibiscus flowers, to taste, and let the mixture steep for 2 to 12 hours in the refrigerator. Strain the mix and store it in the refrigerator.

SPEEDBOAT CAPTAIN

BOAT DRINKS
56 ST GEORGE STREET, ST. AUGUSTINE

This drink is a delicious pick-me-up that is more beach-ready and crushable than an Espresso Martini. It was inspired by a regular guest at the bar who always orders a nonalcoholic version.

GLASSWARE: Collins glass
GARNISH: Lemon peel

- 1½ oz. El Dorado 5 Year Old Rum
- 1½ oz. Lemon Syrup (see recipe)
- 1½ oz. cold brew coffee
- 1 oz. Mexican Coca-Cola, to top

1. Combine all of the ingredients, except for the cola, in a cocktail shaker with a little ice and whip-shake.
2. Pour the cocktail into a collins glass. Top with the soda and more ice.
3. Garnish with a lemon peel.

LEMON SYRUP: In a container, combine 2½ oz. fresh lime juice, 2 oz. fresh lemon juice, and 2 oz. Simple Syrup (see recipe on page 14) and stir.

PIÑA COLADA

BOAT DRINKS
56 ST GEORGE STREET, ST. AUGUSTINE

For the best frozen drink consistency in this batch recipe (serves two), place your bottle of rhum agricole in the freezer for at least an hour before using it. And keep all of your other mixers cold. "We love the interplay between the pure cane flavor profile of the rhum agricole punching through the tropical coconut flavor of real coconut milk," venue co-owner Rob Crabtree says. "We use Thai coconut milk, for its high-fat content—it's the cornerstone of our Piña Colada. You can't, in my opinion, have a good one without really good coconut. So that's what we start, with and then we bolster the drink further with a float of bold Jamaican rum. This is a poolside pounder."

GLASSWARE: Double rocks glass

GARNISH: ½ oz. Worthy Park 109 Jamaica Rum, pineapple wedge

- 6 oz. Coconut Syrup (see recipe)
- 4 oz. Rhum J.M Agricole Blanc 55%
- 4 oz. pineapple juice
- ½ oz. Worthy Park 109 Jamaica Rum

1. Combine all of the ingredients in a blender with about 4 cups ice and blend. Add more ice for a thicker consistency.
2. Pour the cocktail into double rocks glasses.
3. Garnish each serving with a rum float and a pineapple wedge.

94 — FLORIDA COCKTAILS

COCONUT SYRUP:
Combine 1 (14 oz.) can Thai Kitchen coconut milk, 2 cups sugar, and 1 oz. Clément Mahina Coco Liqueur in a blender and blend until combined.

LA REINA MARGARITA

R HOUSE WYNWOOD
2727 NORTHWEST 2ND AVENUE, MIAMI

Named after the queens who strut the stage during R House's infamous Drag Brunches, La Reina Margarita has all the show-stopping ingredients and spectacle you would expect. This tart layered cocktail quenches the thirst after a long night of bingo at gay-owned Latin restaurant R House, a sweat-soaked South Beach club session, or as an accompaniment to the wildly theatrical brunch show.

GLASSWARE: Rocks glass

GARNISH: Dragon fruit slice, blue orchid

- 1½ oz. Tequila Herradura Silver
- ¾ oz. Passion Reàl Passion Fruit Puree Syrup
- ¾ oz. fresh lime juice
- ½ oz. Pierre Ferrand Dry Curaçao
- Dragon fruit puree, to float

1. Combine all of the ingredients, except for the puree, in a cocktail shaker with ice and shake.

2. Strain the cocktail into a rocks glass and float the puree on top.

3. Garnish with a dragon fruit slice and a blue orchid.

SMOKE IN THE GARDEN

TACOCRAFT TAQUERIA & TEQUILA BAR
4400 NORTH OCEAN DRIVE, LAUDERDALE-BY-THE-SEA

For her Smoke in the Garden cocktail, Tacocraft Taqueria & Tequila Bar beverage director Danielle Falsetto brings the smoke with artisanal mezcal and the garden with floral ingredients and fresh mint.

GLASSWARE: Wineglass

GARNISH: Dehydrated orange wheel, mint sprig

- Tajín, for the rim
- 1 mint sprig
- 2 oz. Del Maguey Vida Clásico
- 1½ oz. Hibiscus Syrup (see recipe)
- 1 oz. St-Germain Elderflower Liqueur
- 1 oz. fresh lime juice

1. Wet half the rim of a wineglass then dip the glass in Tajín to give it a rim.
2. Muddle the mint in a cocktail shaker then add the remaining ingredients to the shaker and shake with ice.
3. Strain the cocktail over fresh ice into the rimmed wineglass.
4. Garnish with a dehydrated orange wheel and mint sprig.

HIBISCUS SYRUP: In a medium saucepan over medium heat, combine 1 cup water, 1 cup sugar, and ½ cup dried hibiscus flowers and slowly bring the mixture to a boil. Once at a boil, reduce the heat and simmer for 10 to 15 minutes, stirring often to dissolve the sugar. Remove from heat and allow the mixture to cool. Strain.

GUAVA MAMA

This South Florida hot spot is known for their Margaritas, but when beverage director Danielle Falsetto developed the menu, she employed some alternative flavors that speak to the beach as well as abundant fresh tropical produce and also accommodate Florida's rum obsession.

GLASSWARE: Wineglass

GARNISH: 4 lime wheels

- **2 oz. Bacardí Superior White Rum**
- **1 oz. St-Germain Elderflower Liqueur**
- **1 oz. fresh lime juice**
- **1 oz. guava puree**

1. Combine all of the ingredients in a cocktail shaker with ice and shake.
2. Garnish by lining the inside of a wineglass with lime wheels.
3. Strain the cocktail over fresh ice.

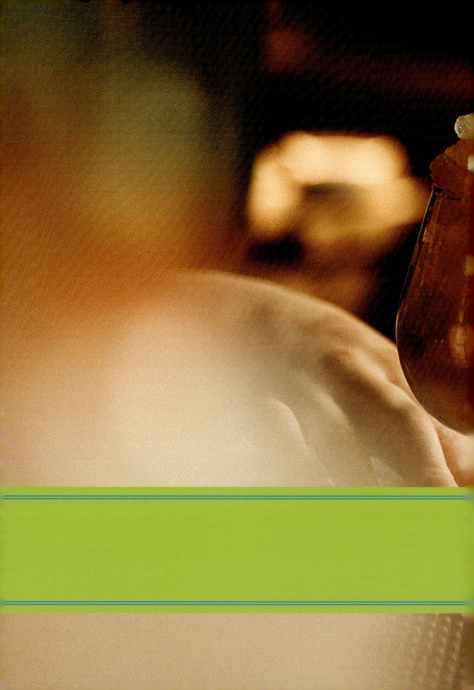

CLASSICS REMIXED

NIKHIL ABUVALA, DAYTRADER TIKI

Florida offers the perfect setting for tropical cocktails, and one of the classic tropical cocktails, the Mai Tai, is making a comeback. A rum-based cocktail hailing from America's mid-century escapist wave, when tiki bars flourished from Hawaii to California to Florida, the Mai Tai nose-dived in quality in the dark days of cocktail culture, the 1980s, when non-fresh and overly sweet ingredients and vividly colorful pre-made mixes ruled the cocktail landscape.

But now that we're well into the cocktail renaissance of the twenty-first century, tiki enthusiasts have recovered the original recipes that celebrated fresh juices, simple preparation, and good-quality rum. At Daytrader Tiki in Seaside, a beach community on Florida's Panhandle, Nikhil Abuvala gets a little playful with his version. "I wanted to bring it closer to the original concept of tiki, where everything was balanced and fresh, down to the sugarcane juice," he says.

Abuvala got inspiration for his serving vessel at a Halloween party in Palm Beach. The cocktail he ordered came out in a blood bag, and he knew this was something he wanted to incorporate into his vision for Daytrader, where clocking out of reality and clocking into escape would be his throughline. "We're in Florida, you know. We're on the beach, it's a bright, beautiful place, but we're not in Hawaii and I'm not Hawaiian. It was important to me to execute this concept without cultural appropriation. We eliminated traditional-style tiki mugs with the totems and religious iconography and went with vintage glass-ware that still feels like an homage to tiki but without cultural appropriation."

THE REMEDY

DAYTRADER TIKI
2236 EAST COUNTY HIGHWAY 30A UNIT 4 & 5, SEASIDE

Gregory Genias, better known as "Bootleg Greg," was hired by Nikhil Abuvala to consult on the bar program for Daytrader. Bootleg Greg's grandfather was part of the rum-running operations between Jamaica and the United States during Prohibition, and under Bootleg Greg's direction, the Mai Tai transformed into The Remedy, a blend of passion fruit syrup, pineapple juice, fresh lime juice, orgeat, and the original rum. Honoring the original recipe while adding an edgy presentation, Abuvala serves the dramatic IV bag of punch over a glass of ice with a single sprig of fresh mint as a garnish.

GLASSWARE: Double rocks glass

GARNISH: Freshly grated nutmeg, mint sprig, pineapple wedge

- ½ oz. passion fruit syrup
- ½ oz. fresh lime juice
- ¼ oz. orgeat
- 1 oz. fresh orange juice
- 1 oz. fresh pineapple juice
- 2 oz. aged Jamaican rum
- 1 oz. Wray & Nephew White Overproof Rum
- 3 dashes Fee Brothers Cranberry Bitters

1. In a shaker tin, build the cocktail by adding the ingredients in the order listed.
2. Add ice and shake well.
3. Strain the cocktail over ice into a double rocks glass.
4. Garnish with a fresh grating of nutmeg, mint sprig, and a pineapple wedge.

SO FRESH & CLEAN

DAYTRADER TIKI
2236 EAST COUNTY HIGHWAY 30A UNIT 4 & 5, SEASIDE

Nikhil Abuvala considers the So Fresh & Clean to be his signature cocktail. "For me, it's what I want on a bright sunny day," he says, "refreshing cucumber juice, tangy lime juice, a little simple syrup, and ChainBridge Florida Basil Vodka. This drink honors my ethos of sticking to small producers based in Florida. They are a tiny, family-operated distillery in Fort Lauderdale that uses fresh ingredients, making their spirits intensely flavorful."

GLASSWARE: Coupe glass

GARNISH: Skewered cucumber ribbon, fresh basil sprig

- 1 oz. Simple Syrup (see recipe on page 14)
- 1 oz. fresh lime juice
- 1 oz. Cucumber Extract (see recipe)
- 2 oz. ChainBridge Florida Basil Vodka

1. Chill a coupe glass. Combine all of the ingredients, in the order listed, in a cocktail shaker with ice and shake vigorously.

2. Double-strain the cocktail into the chilled coupe.

3. Garnish with a slim cucumber ribbon skewered with a basil sprig.

Cucumber Extract: Combine 1 large cucumber, with the skin, and 1 cup water in a blender and blend on high for 15 seconds. Strain.

A BEACH BUM IN MOSCOW

DAYTRADER TIKI
2236 EAST COUNTY HIGHWAY 30A UNIT 4 & 5, SEASIDE

You might say this tastes like a Cape Cod and Moscow Mule had a really adorable baby, and that would be correct. Owner Nikhil Abuvala adds some lemonade for little pucker factor. At his flamingo-hued tiki bar in Seaside, he serves these up in a shareable conch shell like a punch of old.

GLASSWARE: Conch shell

GARNISH: Rubber duckie, mint sprig

- 4 oz. cranberry juice
- 3 oz. Distillery 98 Half Shell Vodka
- 2 oz. lemonade
- 3 mint leaves
- 3 oz. ginger beer, to top

1. Combine all of the ingredients, in the order listed, except for the ginger beer, in a cocktail shaker with ice and shake well.
2. Strain the cocktail over fresh ice into a conch shell and top with the ginger beer.
3. Garnish with a mint sprig and a rubber duckie.

SPICY GARDEN-RITA

DAYTRADER TIKI
2236 EAST COUNTY HIGHWAY 30A UNIT 4 & 5, SEASIDE

This version of a Spicy Margarita adds an interesting twist: pawpaw. North America's tropical fruit, it is indigenous to the continental United States and has a bold tropical flavor that has notes of mango and banana and a hint of tangy passion fruit. During their season, they can be found all over farmers markets in Florida.

GLASSWARE: Collins glass

GARNISH: Dehydrated lime wheel, mint sprig, pineapple leaf

- 3 large chunks pineapple
- 1 packed cup spinach
- 2 oz. Pueblo Viejo Blanco Tequila
- ½ oz. fresh lime juice
- ½ oz. fresh orange juice
- ¼ oz. agave nectar
- ¼ oz. Munyon's Paw-Paw Premium Florida Liqueur
- 1 sprig cilantro
- 6 mint leaves
- 1 jalapeño slice

1. Combine all of the ingredients in a blender with 1 cup ice and blend on high until smooth, about 20 seconds.
2. Pour the cocktail into a collins glass.
3. Garnish with a dehydrated lime wheel, mint sprig, and pineapple leaf.

DECONSTRUCTED MIAMI VICE

THE OYSTER SOCIETY
599 SOUTH COLLIER BOULEVARD #218, MARCO ISLAND

A fixture at beach bars around Florida, the Miami Vice—the love child of a frozen Piña Colada and a Strawberry Daiquiri—gets its name from the hit 1980s TV show in which detectives Crockett and Tubbs's collection of pastel suits captivated viewers as they raced around Miami in sports cars. The cocktail was born out of the frozen batch cocktail craze of the 1980s, and today, whether the two contributing cocktails are swirled together, layered, or candy-cane-style striped, the Miami Vice endures.

GLASSWARE: Collins glass

GARNISH: Piña Colada Foam (see recipe), raspberry powder

- 1 oz. Coconut Fat-Washed Tequila (see recipe)
- 1 oz. Planteray Stiggins' Fancy Pineapple Rum
- 1 oz. lemon juice
- ½ oz. Pineapple Cordial (see recipe)
- ½ oz. Strawberry Cordial (see recipe)

1. Combine all of the ingredients in a cocktail shaker with ice and shake.
2. Strain the cocktail into a collins glass filled with ice.
3. Garnish with Piña Colada Foam and a dusting of raspberry powder.

COCONUT FAT-WASHED TEQUILA: Add 4 oz. virgin coconut oil, in liquid form, to 1 liter silver tequila in a glass jar and let the infusion rest at room temperature for 6 hours. Then place it in the freezer overnight. Strain the tequila to remove the solidified coconut oil.

PINEAPPLE CORDIAL: In a small saucepan over medium-low heat, combine 1 (6 oz.) can pineapple juice, 5 oz. sugar, and ½ teaspoon vanilla extract and stir until the sugar is dissolved. Allow the cordial to cool.

STRAWBERRY CORDIAL: Combine 6 oz. strawberries, hulled; 16 oz. sugar, and 1 teaspoon vanilla in a vacuum bag and sous vide for 1 hour at 145°F. Strain and discard the solids.

PIÑA COLADA FOAM: In a blender, combine 12 oz. pineapple juice, 13 oz. coconut milk, and 6 oz. Licor 43 and blend at low speed. Put the colada in an iSi canister, charge it twice with nitrogen cartridges, shake the canister, and put it in a cooler for 2 hours before use.

OLA PROVENCE

THE OYSTER SOCIETY
599 SOUTH COLLIER BOULEVARD #218, MARCO ISLAND

This cocktail takes inspiration from the fields of lavender found throughout Provence, in France.

GLASSWARE: Rocks glass

GARNISH: Cucumber ribbon

- 1½ oz. Butterfly Pea Flower–Infused Tequila (see recipe)
- ½ oz. Ancho Reyes Verde Chile Poblano Liqueur
- ½ oz. cucumber juice
- ½ oz. Lavender Syrup (see recipe)
- ¼ oz. fresh lime juice

1. Combine all of the ingredients in a shaker tin with ice and shake.
2. Strain the cocktail into a rocks glass and garnish with a cucumber ribbon.

BUTTERFLY PEA FLOWER–INFUSED TEQUILA: Combine 1 (1 liter) bottle blanco tequila and 24 grams butterfly pea flower in a jar and and let the infusion rest for 30 minutes. Strain the tequila back into its bottle.

LAVENDER SYRUP: In a saucepan over medium-low heat, combine 10 oz. water, 10 oz. sugar, 6 tablespoons dried lavender flowers, the peel from 1 orange, and ½ teaspoon rosewater and bring the mixture to a simmer, stirring until the sugar is dissolves. Remove the syrup from heat and let it sit for 1 hour. Strain and store in the refrigerator.

THE FIELD

THE OYSTER SOCIETY
599 SOUTH COLLIER BOULEVARD #218,
MARCO ISLAND

This cocktail tastes like spring in a glass. Pair it with clean, briny oysters or any other springy dish you love.

GLASSWARE: Coupe glass

GARNISH: Rosebuds, Angostura bitters

- 1½ oz. Jasmine Green Tea Gin (see recipe)
- ¾ oz. egg white
- ½ oz. Lavender Syrup (see recipe on page 114)
- ½ oz. St-Germain Elderflower Liqueur
- ¼ oz. fresh lime juice
- 4 to 6 drops Peychaud's bitters

1. Combine all of the ingredients in a cocktail shaker and dry-shake.
2. Add ice and shake again.
3. Strain the cocktail into a coupe.
4. Garnish with rosebuds and Angostura bitters.

JASMINE GREEN TEA GIN: In a large jar, combine 4 bags jasmine green tea and 1 (1 liter) bottle of gin. Let the infusion steep for 10 minutes. Remove the tea bags and rebottle.

ALEX APORTELA, AMELIA'S 1931

Alex Aportela, beverage director for Amelia's 1931, located in the West Kendall neighborhood of Miami, understands flavor. He went to culinary school but floundered as he neared graduation. A friend suggested bartending as he figured out a career path. Now, over fourteen years later, and with some encouragement from chef Eileen Andrade, he leans on his culinary training and understanding of ingredients to drive the beverage program at Amelia's 1931. "We like to push boundaries at Amelia's," he says. "We aren't scared or discouraged to try different things. If it fails, we try something different, until we land on what works. Sometimes it means utilizing dairy to clarify the cocktail for better texture, or maybe it is employing a Peruvian pepper for an infusion that sparks the rest of the ingredients in the drink."

MACHU PIKACHU

AMELIA'S 1931
13601 SOUTHWEST 26TH STREET, MIAMI

Renowned bartender Sam Ross invented The London (sometimes called Old Maid) cocktail in 2004 at Milk & Honey in New York. The technique behind it became one of the defining hallmarks of the craft cocktail renaissance of the twenty-first century, and a slew of "Maids" entered the scene, including the inspiration for Amelia's 1931 beverage director Alex Aportela's Machu Pikachu cocktail. "I immediately thought of the aji amarillo, a Peruvian pepper that's not too peppery or spicy but has a distinctive flavor. 'Maids' are usually made with fresh mint, but I wanted a more earthy, vibrant wow factor, so I added fresh sage. We still added a little bit of salt, and then came my favorite ingredient, Yellow Chartreuse, for that bold color." With supplies dwindling, a good substitute for Yellow Chartreuse is Liquore Strega.

GLASSWARE: Rocks glass

GARNISH: Fruit leather, mint sprig

- 1½ oz. Aji Amarillo-Infused Tequila (see recipe)
- ½ oz. Yellow Chartreuse
- ¾ oz. fresh lime juice
- ½ oz. fresh cucumber juice
- ½ oz. Simple Syrup (see recipe on page 14)
- 1 fresh sage leaf
- Pinch salt

1. Chill a rocks glass. Combine all of the ingredients in a cocktail shaker tin and fill the tin three-fourths of the way with ice.

2. Shake for about 6 to 8 seconds.

3. Double-strain the cocktail into the chilled rocks glass over chip ice.

4. Garnish with a fresh mint sprig and fruit leather.

AJI AMARILLO-INFUSED TEQUILA: In 1 (750 ml) bottle of your favorite premium tequila, steep aji amarillo peppers, to taste, for 48 hours. Strain and rebottle.

DR. BEET

Alex Aportela employed a unique clarification method to bring Dr. Beet to life. "Clarifying usually involves dairy, but I wanted something vegan-friendly. I used agar-agar, an algae that strips the impurities off all the ingredients, creating a filter so you get a more refined color and taste. If making homemade candy isn't on the menu, grab some apricot fruit chews for a fun, interactive garnish.

GLASSWARE: Collins glass

GARNISH: Soft-chew candy, skewered

- 2 oz. Havana Club Original 86° Proof Añejo Blanco Rum
- 2 oz. Coconut Beet Cordial (see recipe)
- ½ oz. apricot liqueur

1. Combine all of the ingredients in a collins glass with ice and stir. Garnish with soft-chew candy.

COCONUT BEET CORDIAL: In a saucepan, combine 500 ml coconut water, 250 ml fresh beet juice, and the juice of 2 to 3 limes. Sprinkle 20 grams agar-agar flakes or powder evenly over the liquid mixture. Stir gently to incorporate the agar-agar. Place the saucepan over medium heat and bring the mixture to a gentle boil while stirring continuously. This helps dissolve the agar-agar. Reduce the heat and simmer for 5 to 7 minutes, stirring until the mixture thickens. Add about 200 grams granulated sugar gradually, stirring continuously until the cordial reaches your desired level of sweetness. Add 1 to 2 tablespoons rum or vodka, optional, to preserve the cordial for longer.

YASS QUEEN

Alex Aportela took inspiration from his surroundings when developing the Yass Queen. "Amelia's 1931 has a very Prohibition look, with antique finishes. I wanted to incorporate antique glassware and it turned into a very tea-forward cocktail. The Earl Grey gives it elegant floral notes, and the vodka is neutral and brings out the best in the tea. When you drink this cocktail and look around the restaurant, it transports you to the 1930s, the time when Chef Eileen Andrade's grandmother [and inspiration for the restaurant] was born."

GLASSWARE: Vintage teacup

GARNISH: Ardbeg Ten Years Old mist; whole nutmeg, grated

- 2 oz. Earl Grey–Infused Vodka (see recipe)
- ¾ oz. fresh lemon juice
- ½ oz. St. Elizabeth Allspice Dram
- ¼ oz. orange blossom honey

1. Combine all of the ingredients with ice in a cocktail shaker and shake.
2. Strain the cocktail into a teacup with ice.
3. To garnish, mist the scotch over the cocktail and grate fresh nutmeg over the top.

EARL GREY–INFUSED VODKA: In a large, clean glass container with a lid, combine 1 (750 ml) bottle of Haku Vodka and 2 grams Earl Grey tea leaves. Seal and shake the jar gently and allow the infusion to sit for 2 to 4 hours. Strain the vodka through a fine-mesh strainer or cheesecloth, using a wooden spoon to press the liquid from the leaves, and rebottle.

CHRIS TRULL, WILD CHILD

Bartender Chris Trull was the North American winner of the Indie Bartender Fund competition in 2023. This victory granted him the opportunity to showcase his talents at Cartagena bar Alquímico, a world-renowned bar known for sustainability and named World's Best Bar at the 2024 Tales of the Cocktail Foundation Spirited Awards.

Trull now has over fifteen years of experience behind the bar. He is also a Certified Specialist of Spirits through the Society of Wine Educators, a USBG World Class US 2024 Top 30 Bartender, and a cocktail consultant. But most nights you can find him behind the bar at Wild Child in St. Pete. His cocktails embrace native ingredients like juicy Plant City strawberries, Florida orange blossom honey, and tobacco while taking inspiration from classic drinks like the Daiquiri and adding beachy flavors or his nod to the Irish coffee, Ybor City style.

I DO WATERCOLORS

Bartender Chris Trull wanted to create a drinkable version of Florida's strawberry fields and orange groves. "The state is known for its key limes, oranges, and grapefruit, but many do not know that Florida has some of the best strawberries in the world," he says. "Every spring, Plant City hosts the Florida Strawberry Festival, an agriculture fair held by the Florida Department of Agriculture that draws thousands of visitors to highlight all things strawberry." To finish I Do Watercolors, Trull creates a cloud of orange blossom air that brings the scents of the orange grove to the presentation.

GLASSWARE: Nick & Nora glass

GARNISH: Orange Blossom Air (see recipe)

- 1¾ oz. St. George Valley Gin
- ¼ oz. Lacto Strawberry & Rhubarb (see recipe)
- ¼ oz. Italicus Rosolio di Bergamotto
- ¾ oz. Roasted Fennel Honey (see recipe)
- ¾ oz. fresh lemon juice

1. Chill a Nick & Nora glass. Combine all of the ingredients in a cocktail shaker, add ice, and shake.
2. Fine-strain the cocktail into the chilled Nick & Nora. Garnish with Orange Blossom Air.

LACTO STRAWBERRY & RHUBARB: Remove the tops of the strawberries from 2 packages of strawberries, roughly chop 6 stalks of rhubarb, and combine them in a bowl. Weigh the mixture. Calculate 2% of that total weight. Add the fruits to a blender with 2% of the weight of Maldon Sea Salt Flakes and blend. Vacuum seal the blended mixture in a vacuum bag for 5 to 6 days, checking each day that the expanding bag does not burst. Carefully de-gas the top corner of the vacuum bag by cutting it with scissors. Fine-strain the mixture, bottle it, and store it in the refrigerator for no more than 2 weeks.

ROASTED FENNEL HONEY: Cut 1 fennel bulb in half. Place the fennel bulb halves on a baking sheet lined with foil or baking paper and roast at 450°F for 15 to 25 minutes. Remove the bulb from the oven and let it cool. Combine 500 grams honey syrup and the roasted fennel bulb in a vacuum bag. Seal with a vacuum sealer, or use the submersion method and add it to a sous vide bath at 136.4°F (62.5°C) for 2 hours. Fine-strain the mixture, let it cool, and bottle it. Refrigerate and use within 2 weeks.

ORANGE BLOSSOM AIR: Add 300 grams water to a quart container. Add 5 dashes of orange blossom or orange flower water. Weigh 0.4% to 0.6%, or 1.5 grams, lecithin and add it to the quart. Cover the container and shake. When needed, add an air stone with an aerator pump to the quart to inflate the air. Remove the air stone when not in use. Once inflated, use a julep strainer to scoop out the desired amount of air. Place the bubble on top of the finished cocktail.

CAFÉ DE TRANVÍA

This cocktail is based on the classic Irish Coffee, with a distinctive Ybor City twist. The café Cubano, a strong, espresso-like coffee, can be found all over Ybor City. Bartender Chris Trull says, "By including café Cubano in the cocktail, I'd like to capture that same essence of community and open dialogue, of sharing not only a coffee and conversation, but now a cocktail—and the soul of the city itself." The name, Café de Tranvía, was inspired by the streetcars that operated between Tampa and Ybor City, beginning in 1885 with wood-burning steam engines. The streetcar system in the Tampa area grew to an extensive network but was shut down in 1949. They've returned, albeit in a more limited scope.

GLASSWARE: Irish coffee glass

GARNISH: Coconut Dulce de Leche (see recipe), 3 espresso beans

- 1½ oz. Bacardí Reserva Ocho
- ⅓ oz. Florida Orange Blossom Honey Syrup (see recipe)
- ⅓ oz. Sandalwood-Infused Sherry (see recipe)
- 4 dashes Fee Brothers Turkish Tobacco Bitters
- 2 drops Saline Solution (see recipe on page 14)
- 3 oz. freshly brewed café Cubano

1. Preheat an Irish coffee glass with hot water and set aside.
2. Combine all of the ingredients, except for the coffee, in a mixing glass and stir to combine.
3. Discard the water from the coffee glass, then pour in the mixed cocktail and the coffee and stir to combine.
4. Garnish with Coconut Dulce de Leche and 3 espresso beans.

FLORIA ORANGE BLOSSOM HONEY SYRUP: Combine 150 grams Florida orange blossom honey and 96 grams (96 ml) 135°F water in a container and stir.

SANDALWOOD-INFUSED SHERRY: Combine 4 oz. amontillado sherry and 4.5 grams food-grade sandalwood in a vacuum bag (or sealable bag). Place the bag in a 135°F (57.7°C) sous vide bath for 2 hours. Allow the mixture to cool, then fine-strain, bottle, and keep it in the refrigerator for up to 3 weeks. Alternatively, use a mason jar and infuse in the refrigerator for 72 hours.

COCONUT DULCE DE LECHE:
Whisk 1 (14 oz.) can unsweetened coconut milk, ¼ cup demerara sugar, and 1 pinch coarse salt in a large skillet over medium heat until the sugar dissolves. Increase the heat to medium-high and boil until the mixture is reduced to 1¼ cups, stirring occasionally, about 20 to 40 minutes. Remove the mixture from heat. Mix in 3 tablespoons (23.5 grams) soy lecithin. Add 15 dashes of Fee Brothers Fee Foam. Allow the dulce de leche to cool overnight. Add it to a cream whipper and charge twice, shaking vigorously between charges. Place the cream whipper in a cool sous vide bath and slowly bring the temperature up to 140°F. Shake before use.

MINT SIMPLE SYRUP: Combine 25⅓ oz. (750 ml) water and 25⅓ oz. (750 ml) sugar in a pot and simmer gently until the sugar is dissolved. Combine the simple syrup and 100 grams fresh mint in a Vitamix (or blender) and blend for 20 seconds. Strain any solids through a chinois. Let the syrup cool. Transfer to a quart container and label.

SCUBA STEVE

THE WELL
42 EAST GARDEN STREET, PENSACOLA

S cuba Steve has been on the menu at The Well, a Pensacola cocktail lounge that exudes 1950s Miami style, since day one. Beverage director Alex Broz wanted to take the traditional Moscow Mule in a subaquatic direction. "You get your spice, your sweetness, and, visually, it's a beautiful drink," Broz says. They now serve this cocktail in a snifter, but ask to see the hammered copper diver cup with porthole they served Scuba Steve in when they opened.

GLASSWARE: Snifter glass
GARNISH: Cucumber slice, mint sprig

- 1½ oz. Reyka Vodka
- 1 oz. cucumber juice
- ½ oz. Mint Simple Syrup (see recipe)
- ½ oz. fresh lime juice
- ¼ oz. blue curaçao
- Ginger beer, to top

1. Combine all of the ingredients, except for the ginger beer, in a cocktail shaker with ice and shake.
2. Strain the cocktail into a snifter filled with crushed ice. Top with ginger beer.
3. Garnish with a cucumber slice and fresh mint sprig.

PUNCH & JUDY

Punch and Judy, the puppet comedy show originating in seventeenth-century Britain, came to the United States in 1783, first landing in Fell's Point, Maryland. It traveled throughout the mid-Atlantic, its one-man puppeteer show depicting scenes between Mr. Punch and his wife, Judy. The Well's Punch & Judy, a play on words, showcases a riff on a clarified Milk Punch with showstopping visuals. Like other clarified cocktails, this one is strained through milk to pull the proteins from the drink, creating a vibrant pink cocktail. "We took it in the direction of a funky tiki cocktail, but clarified. That smoothed out the powerful flavors and gave it a silky texture that is surprisingly easy to drink," beverage director Alex Broz says.

GLASSWARE: Stemmed rocks glass

GARNISH: Lemon peel

- 1 oz. Avuá Prata Cachaça
- ¾ oz. chamomile tea
- ¾ oz. fresh lime juice
- ½ oz. Guava Hops Syrup (see recipe)
- ¼ oz. dry curaçao
- ¼ oz. Campari
- Whole milk, as needed

1. Combine all of the ingredients in a container to clarify and let the punch sit in the refrigerator overnight.

2. Strain the batch, through the milk curds multiple times, using a fine-mesh strainer lined with cheesecloth until you get a transparent texture.

3. Pour the clarified punch into a mixing glass with ice and stir. Strain the cocktail into a stemmed rocks glass.

4. To garnish, express a lemon peel over the drink and rub the peel around the rim before dropping into drink.

GUAVA HOPS SYRUP: Combine 2 cups sugar and 2 cups water in a pot and simmer until the sugar dissolves. Reduce the heat and add 2 cups hop pellets. Let the mixture steep for 20 to 30 minutes. Strain the syrup through cheesecloth. Measure your yield and add equally as much guava puree by volume and stir.

VELVET FUZZ

THE WELL
42 EAST GARDEN STREET, PENSACOLA

The Velvet Fuzz takes the flavors of your favorite Southern peach cobbler and combines them in a glass. The layers of vanilla, peach puree, and Licor 43's citrus and vanilla notes bring you right back to the orchards and freshly picked peaches. The egg white creates a lovely foam on top, almost like a meringue that seals the sweet-treat vibe of this cocktail.

GLASSWARE: Rocks glass
GARNISH: Lemon zest

- 1 oz. Stoli Vanilla
- ¾ oz. fresh lemon juice
- ½ oz. peach puree
- ¼ oz. Licor 43
- 1 egg white

1. Combine all of the ingredients in a cocktail shaker with ice and shake.
2. Strain the cocktail into a rocks glass filled with crushed ice.
3. Garnish with a lemon zest.

COLD BREW MARTINI

THE WELL
42 EAST GARDEN STREET, PENSACOLA

Beverage director Alex Broz calls this riff on an Espresso Martini his crowd favorite. He uses a Pensacola cold brew concentrate, Mrs. Jones Cold Brew, for the base of this cocktail. "We found that the proteins from the coffee concentrate create that same head as an espresso would but with silky, smooth flavor," he said. "We love sourcing locally, and this delicious cocktail is one people order again and again and again."

GLASSWARE: Nick & Nora glass
GARNISH: 3 coffee beans

- 1½ oz. Bols Vodka
- 1½ oz. cold brew concentrate
- ½ oz. Demerara Syrup (see recipe)

1. Combine all of the ingredients in a cocktail shaker with ice and shake.
2. Double-strain the cocktail into a Nick & Nora.
3. Garnish with three coffee beans.

DEMERARA SYRUP: Make Simple Syrup (see recipe on page 14) but use demerara sugar in place of white granulated sugar.

Sister Hen Speakeasy, Pensacola

PASSCODE, PLEASE

The mystique of speakeasy culture flourishes today with increasingly elaborate entry requirements and themed spaces. Across Florida, you can find candy stores, taco bars, bookshelves, and other disguises fronting dark, mysterious drinking establishments with high-octane cocktails that keep the Prohibition era alive.

A.J. GALECKI, SISTER HEN SPEAKEASY

The first sign is the pay phone outside that doesn't take outgoing calls. The second is the dimly lit side entrance you see down a flight of concrete stairs. The third is that there are no markings or signage. Nevertheless, you have arrived at Sister Hen Speakeasy.

Located in the basement of Lily Hall in Pensacola, a building once threatened with demolition after Hurricane Ivan, Sister Hen occupies what was the Bible school of the former Mount Olive Baptist Church.

A.J. Galecki, the bar manager at Sister Hen, started his bartending journey in the flair-wreathed halls of TGI Fridays. "I was sitting at a bar one day watching two bartenders have fun making drinks. I hated my IT job, so I went to the bookstore, picked up *Death & Co: Modern Classic Cocktails*, read it, set up a bar at my house, and dove in," Galecki says.

Galecki made his rounds in the Pensacola bar scene, barbacking, tending bar, and eventually managing a high-volume cocktail bar. Another chance encounter at a bar led to Sister Hen. "A chef I knew told me they were opening the first speakeasy in town and asked me to come check it out. It was legit," he says.

He put the bones together—flickering candles, the scent of amber and sandalwood filling the space, and eclectic vintage glassware lining the shelves. "I've never worked at a bar where we used antique glassware, and I love it," he says. "We go to the antique shop every couple of months to get similar glasses, but no two are the same, and they are all older than me."

Though the venue is small—they allow only twenty guests at a time—Sister Hen has a twenty-seven-drink menu. "When you go into a good speakeasy, you forget what time it is. You forget where you are," he says. "People tell me every day that they can't believe this is Pensacola. It feels like New York or some other big city, and that always makes me feel like we're doing our job."

GINGER SYRUP: Blend 450 grams cane sugar, 450 grams (450 ml) water, and 200 grams fresh ginger in a food processor. Strain, bottle, and store the syrup in the refrigerator.

DEATH TO INFLATION

S ister Hen bar manager A.J. Galecki took inspiration from the classic cocktail Death in the Afternoon. The absinthe-and-champagne classic shares its name with Ernest Hemingway's 1932 story about Spanish bullfighting and is rumored to have been created by Hemingway during his expatriate days in Paris and Spain. In the recipe notes, Hemingway writes, "Pour one jigger absinthe into a Champagne glass. Add iced Champagne until it attains the proper opalescent milkiness. Drink three to five of these slowly." Galecki adds a few other ingredients to his riff, but the showstopper is the sugar paper $100 bills he sets on fire as a garnish. The phones come out to capture the spectacle as the scent of burning marshmallows fills the cozy bar.

GLASSWARE: Champagne flute
GARNISH: Sugar paper $100 bills, set on fire

- ½ oz. absinthe
- ½ oz. Green Chartreuse
- ½ oz. fresh lime juice
- ½ oz. Ginger Syrup (see recipe)
- Champagne, to top

1. Combine all of the ingredients, except for the champagne, in a cocktail shaker with ice and shake.
2. Strain the cocktail into a champagne flute and top with champagne.
3. Garnish with sugar paper $100 bills and light them on fire.

ARCADIA

SISTER HEN SPEAKEASY
415 NORTH ALCANIZ STREET, PENSACOLA

S ister Hen bar manager A.J. Galecki wanted to develop something inspired by brunch served on the weekends at their neighboring restaurant, Brother Fox. "We wanted to use the opened leftover bottles of champagne from bottomless Mimosas more effectively, so we created our own fancy version of a strawberry-and-bubbles cocktail to sell throughout the week."

GLASSWARE: Pilsner glass

GARNISH: Fresh mint sprig, strawberry slice

- 1½ oz. vodka
- ¾ oz. Strawberry-Orange Champagne Reduction Syrup (see recipe)
- ¾ oz. lemon juice
- ½ oz. St-Germain Elderflower Liqueur

1. Combine all of the ingredients in a cocktail shaker with ice and shake.

2. Strain the cocktail into a pilsner glass.

3. Top with more bubbles and crushed ice. Garnish with fresh mint and a strawberry slice.

STRAWBERRY-ORANGE CHAMPAGNE REDUCTION SYRUP:
In a saucepan, combine 1 pint strawberries with 1 or 2 bottles of champagne and simmer, and reducing the mixture down until the alcohol is cooked off. Add 2 oz. orange juice, strain, weigh the mixture, add an equal part by weight of cane sugar, and stir until the sugar is dissolved. Allow the syrup to cool.

SAIGON SUMMER

SISTER HEN SPEAKEASY
415 NORTH ALCANIZ STREET, PENSACOLA

The Sister Hen team often visits their favorite local bahn mi shop before work. The Saigon Summer brings the pickled flavors and umami of the sandwich in cocktail form. They make pickles in-house, but pickled carrots from the grocery store will do if you are not up for making a quick pickle at home.

GLASSWARE: Rocks glass

GARNISH: Cucumber spiral, pickled carrots, fresh cilantro sprig

- 2 oz. St. George Green Chile Vodka
- ¾ oz. fresh lime juice
- ½ oz. cucumber melon white balsamic vinegar
- ½ oz. Dolin Dry Vermouth
- 2 sprigs cilantro

1. Combine all of the ingredients in a cocktail shaker with ice and shake.
2. Strain the cocktail over ice into a rocks glass.
3. Garnish with a cucumber spiral, pickled carrots, and a sprig of fresh cilantro.

CLARIFIED DREAMSICLE

SISTER HEN SPEAKEASY
415 NORTH ALCANIZ STREET, PENSACOLA

This oranges-and-cream-flavored cocktail comes straight from Sister Hen bar manager A.J. Galecki's childhood. "As kids in the heat of Florida, dreamsicle popsicles were always a cornerstone of our diet. We wanted to make a fun version for adults that reminds of those hot summer days," he says. Galecki also took inspiration with ingredients from the Spanish restaurant next door, Brother Fox. They make this in batches of four servings at a time since the clarification takes twenty-four hours. You can substitute vanilla ice cream or orange sorbet for the garnish.

GLASSWARE: Collins glass

GARNISH: Earl Grey Vanilla Cold Foam (see recipe)

- 5½ oz. Rives Spanish Gin
- 3 oz. orange juice
- 2 oz. fresh lemon juice
- 2 oz. Licor 43
- 2 oz. Earl Grey Vanilla Syrup (see recipe)
- 2 oz. water
- 6 oz. whole milk

1. In a nonreactive container, combine all of the ingredients in the order listed and stir well. Cover the container and refrigerate overnight.

2. Strain the punch through a fine-mesh strainer lined with a coffee filter. The first ounce or so will be cloudy; simply pour the cloudy part back into the mix and strain it again.

3. The curdled milk settles into the filter and forms a third filter, resulting in a clear (clarified) cocktail.

4. Pour the cocktail into a collins glass over clear ice.

5. Garnish with the foam.

EARL GREY VANILLA SYRUP: Steep 15 grams Earl Grey tea in 450 grams (450 ml) hot water for 20 minutes. Remove the tea, and add 450 grams cane sugar, stirring until the sugar is dissolved. Add 3 barspoons vanilla extract and stir. Bottle the syrup and store it in the refrigerator.

EARL GREY VANILLA COLD FOAM: Combine 8 oz. half-and-half, 6 oz. Earl Grey Vanilla Syrup (see recipe), and 4 oz. vodka in a 1-pint N_2O whipped cream canister. Deploy.

SUNSHINE STATE SPEAKEASIES

PANGEA ALCHEMY LAB
1564 MAIN STREAT, SARASOTA

Boozy cereal bowls served with spiked milk? Yes, please! If the nod to childhood favorites Frosted Flakes and Fruit Loops doesn't draw you in, the specialty infusions, tinctures, syrups, and creams they mix up here will. Tucked away in an alley behind Main Street, a nondescript door opens to a vintage bulb–lit interior where industrial design meets century-old exposed brick. Pangea Alchemy Lab serves up creative cocktails alongside tasty bites like cauliflower tempura and barbacoa sandwiches. They also have an entire menu devoted to absinthe.

THE GREEN HAT
5300 POWERLINE ROAD, FORT LAUDERDALE

Getting to this speakeasy is like unpacking Russian nesting dolls— inside Xtreme Action Park are the Evolution Escape Rooms, where a door with a code that changes weekly reveals The Green Hat speakeasy. The green-hued bar boasts a kitschy menu of cocktails inspired by the story of notorious bootlegger James Cassidy and his green fedora. A rumrunner in South Florida, Cassidy smuggled illegal alcohol from the Bahamas to South Florida aboard his speedboat, *The Leviathan* (one of the drinks on the menu). He evaded the U.S. Coast Guard until a run may have taken him headfirst into a tropical storm. After the storm, a piece of wood bearing the words "The Leviathan" drifted into the Coast Guard's possession and the man in the green hat was presumed dead. But that's when sightings of a mythological man wearing a green fedora, including by hunters in the swamps of Florida who said they saw a man in a green fedora living off the land, perpetuated Cassidy's legend. Drinks like the Stowaway, the Parlay, and their signature Green Hat Grogg pay homage to the rumrunner.

The Green Hat

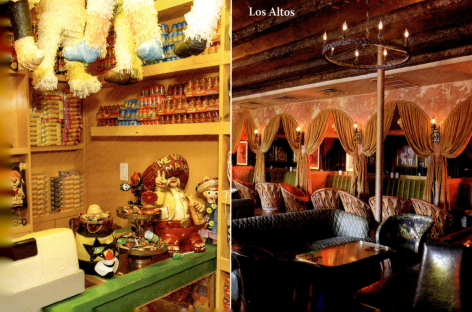

Los Altos

LOS ALTOS
521 SOUTHWEST 8TH STREET, MIAMI

Above Taquerias el Mexicano in Little Havana, up the stairs behind a false wall inside a Mexican candy shop, sits Los Altos. Inside you'll find velvet banquettes, hand-painted tiles, a gold-leaf ceiling, thick curtains, dim red lighting, and a collection of Mexican art paying homage to Aztec gods and goddesses. The cocktail program takes its cue from authentic Mexican drinking culture.

HIDDEN SPEAKEASY
4134 NORTH FEDERAL HIGHWAY, FORT LAUDERDALE

A door labeled "pantry" inside a restaurant called Eatapas in Fort Lauderdale leads to a space filled with ambient lighting, dark leather couches, and Prohibition-era decor. Hidden Speakeasy offers a range of cocktails, from classics like Martinis and Negronis to new takes like the Chocolate Charlie, which combines coffee-infused rum, hazelnut liqueur, and chocolate mole bitters, garnished with a dark chocolate-covered orange and a maraschino cherry. Jazz music plays in the background, experienced bartenders deftly mix drinks behind the bar, and the mood is sultry at this hidden gem.

ODD BIRDS
200 ANASTASIA BOULEVARD, ST. AUGUSTINE

Just over the bridge from Historic Downtown St. Augustine, on Anastasia Island, a popular Venezuelan-leaning restaurant and craft cocktail bar houses a speakeasy, which is accessed only by opening the Odd Birds book on the bookshelf adjacent to the bar and entering a code. Inside, you will encounter a dimly lit haven with high-octane cocktails.

THE VOLSTEAD
115 WEST ADAMS STREET, JACKSONVILLE

Drawing inspiration from 1920s speakeasies, this lounge hides behind a JAX POST sign in an empty storefront of the W.A. Knight building. Pull back the curtain and you'll find jazz albums from a bygone era spinning and classic craft cocktails expertly made from small-batch spirits and ingredients from the local farmers market.

KAONA ROOM
1600 NORTHEAST 1ST AVENUE, MIAMI

In Miami's Arts & Entertainment District, a discreet door on a condo building, with a buzzer that says "Ring for a Mai-Tai," is your entrance to this "speaky-tiki." For forty-five guests at a time, the Kaona Room serves up the full Polynesian escape with its flaming cocktails, tropical decor, and island music.

DANTE'S HIFI
519 NORTHWEST 26TH STREET, MIAMI

Tucked into a Wynwood courtyard, the only sign you've made it to Dante's HiFi is the music being piped out above a black door. The all-vinyl listening bar boasts nearly 8,500 records, fifty seats (reservation required), and an atmosphere inspired by the listening bars in Japan. The cocktail menu continues the theme, with a heavy emphasis on highballs crafted with Japanese whiskey, but a smattering of beer, wine, and other cocktails also have spots on the menu. If imbibing while enjoying a curated playlist of smooth tunes appeals to you, Dante's is pretty special.

CHECK IN

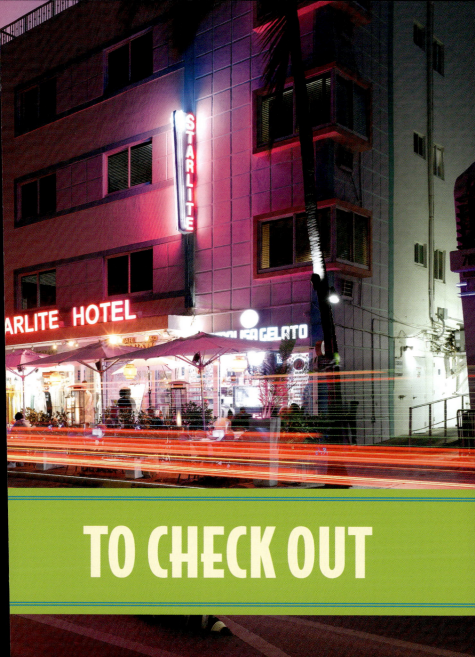

TO CHECK OUT

Historically, hotel bars were the place to go. In the 1800s, they offered a rare amenity: a cold drink when the heat index soared. They boasted refrigeration and ice when it was still too expensive to be widely available. Bars became the selling point as travelers chose hotels, and early barmen put on a show of mixing elegant tipples for their patrons. In the 2000s, after the neon-soaked world of Cocktail-inspired bars faded, hotel bars rose again as ambassadors of their neighborhoods and welcoming homes for travelers. Classic cocktails gained a new legion of fans, and hospitality and service again reigned.

ALEXA DELGADO, THE MATADOR BAR

For Alexa Delgado, bar director at The Miami Beach EDITION hotel, it took a stint as a file clerk in a law firm to reveal her path. She contemplated law school, but didn't like the practice of law. She applied for a master's in food and beverage program in Milan and moved to Italy. She's been in the bartending/mixology business ever since.

"I've opened a Michelin restaurant with Marriott, developing their bar concept," she says. "I've done the Grand Cayman Cookout, hosted by Eric Ripert, four times. Now at The Matador Bar, my focus is to be relevant in the local community while creating an experience that captivates guests at our hotel bars so they don't leave and go to the bar down the street."

Like guests who check in at the hotel, the bartenders at The Matador Bar come from somewhere else, but Delgado is a Miami native. "The Miami Beach community is made up of a very diverse international population. I bite into a watermelon and taste summer in my backyard playing in the sprinklers, but someone else may have the memory of the first bite of watermelon at a roadside stand after finally settling in a free country. We want to bring all those experiences to life in our cocktails. Miami is not just sunshine, beaches, nightclubs, and pretty people in bathing suits—it's home."

Delgado and her team focus on seasonality and house-made syrups and tinctures. They also take inspiration from chef Jean-Georges Vongerichten's Spanish-leaning Matador Room menu—photographs from renowned French photographer Lucien Clergue's *Matador* series hang on the walls, customers nosh Cinco Jotas Jamón and Manchego Cheese Fritters, and thoughtful cocktails like La Hacienda Spritz are sipped at the solid walnut floating bar in the center of the space.

"I'm always thinking of what we can do to leave an indelible mark on our guests, what are they going to take home with them," Delgado says. "Miami is flashy; it's sexy. It's captivating, but it's also me sitting in my friend's kitchen gossiping. The hotel bar offers the opportunity to share each other's stories over a delicious cocktail, creating those memories that will stick even after the guest checks out."

CAT 5

I f you can trace your lineage back three generations, on both sides, to Madrid, Spain, you call yourself Gato, or "Cat" in English. Bartender Florina Bule shares the history of the term: in 1085, when Alfonso VI's armies sought to retake Madrid from Moorish rule, a soldier was said to have climbed the walls, known to be impossible to scale, with only a dagger, like a cat. Then, to carry the cat theme further, bar director Alexa Delgado introduced ceramic cat cups; bartender Michael Berland, known as "Cat Daddy" by his coworkers, suggested a catnip infusion and Harridan Vodka as the base spirit. "The word *harridan* represents a witchy, belligerent woman," says Delgado, "so it played into the idea of seances, covens, spirits, and cats."

GLASSWARE: Ceramic cat cup

GARNISH: Mint sprig, paper pinwheel

- 1½ oz. Harridan Vodka
- ¾ oz. Catnip Syrup (see recipe)
- ½ oz. New Zealand sauvignon blanc
- ½ oz. guava puree
- ¼ oz. fresh lemon juice

1. Combine all of the ingredients in a shaker tin and fill the tin three-fourths of the way with ice. Shake for 10 seconds.

2. Strain the cocktail over fresh ice into a ceramic cat cup.

3. Garnish with a mint sprig and a paper pinwheel.

CATNIP SYRUP: In a saucepan, heat 1 cup water to approximately 170°F (a simmer). Steep ⅓ cup catnip in the water for 4 minutes. Strain out the catnip and return the water to the pot. Add 1 cup sugar and stir, simmering, until the sugar is dissolved. Allow the syrup to cool.

THE BALLER

Looking to add more interactive experiences to her beverage program, bar director Alexa Delgado came up with this ultra-premium cocktail. She enlisted a local ice purveyor to infuse a clear sphere with a gold coin so as it melts the coin is revealed. Also wanting to bring some of her Miami heritage to the drink, she added cafecito, a sweet coffee beloved by Cubans. "It has the flavors of a Miami that not everybody knows," she says. "My grandfather sat around outside drinking his Cuban coffee, smoking a cigar, while playing dominoes. That's what The Baller feels like." Matador bartenders serve it in a smoking box filled with cigar smoke from local tobacco leaves—another nod to Miami's Cuban culture. You need a cocktail smoking setup to pull this off like The Matador Bar does.

GLASSWARE: Double rocks glass

GARNISH: Cigar smoke, Gold Coin Ice Sphere (see recipe)

- 2 oz. Glenfiddich 14 Year Old Bourbon Barrel Reserve
- ¼ oz. Cafecito Syrup (see recipe)
- 3 dashes Bittermens Xocolatl Mole Bitters

1. Chill a mixing glass. Combine all of the ingredients in the chilled mixing glass. Fill the mixing glass three-fourths of the way with ice and stir for 20 seconds.

2. Using a julep strainer, strain the cocktail over a large ice cube into a double rocks glass.

3. Garnish with a Gold Coin Ice Sphere and create your own smoke effect at home with a cloche, using a heat-resistant plate or a smoking board, with the cigar smoke, smoking the glass.

GOLD COIN ICE SPHERE: Freeze a coin, or some other gold (or goldish) object that represents luxury, in an ice cube tray. Pop them out to serve.

CAFECITO SYRUP: Combine equal parts Cuban coffee and sugar and stir.

COCONUT OIL–WASHED CAMPARI: Melt coconut oil, to taste, into liquid form and then combine with 1 (750 ml) bottle of Campari (or use less) in a freezer-safe container and stir. Freeze the mixture overnight; the coconut oil will coagulate on top (it will look like salad dressing left in the refrigerator). Remove the container from the freezer and scrape off the coagulated coconut oil. Strain the Campari through a coffee filter and rebottle it.

TROPICAL NEGRONI

THE MATADOR BAR
2901 COLLINS AVENUE, MIAMI BEACH

Inspired by the Atlantic Ocean and Piña Coladas on the beach, bartender Christopher Galdarez brought this riff on the classic Negroni to life. "This is perfect for sipping while you look at the ocean at night," says bar director Alexa Delagado. "The addition of the pineapple Chris brought to the recipe makes it a little bit lighter and brighter than a classic Negroni. It's such a universal version—it's versatile, but you don't lose the integrity of the drink."

GLASSWARE: Double rocks glass

GARNISH: Orange peel origami

- **1 oz. Pineapple-Infused Gin (see recipe)**

- **1 oz. Coconut Oil–Washed Campari**

- **1 oz. Lo-Fi Sweet Vermouth**

1. Chill a mixing glass. Combine all of the ingredients in the chilled mixing glass. Fill the mixing glass three-fourths of the way with ice and stir for 20 seconds.

2. Using a julep strainer, strain the cocktail over a large ice cube into a double rocks glass.

3. Garnish with orange peel origami.

PINEAPPLE-INFUSED GIN: In a large container, combine 1 (750 ml) bottle of London dry gin and 100 grams fresh pineapple, skins off. Let the infusion sit for 24 hours, then strain and rebottle.

NATHAN BERUMEN, KIMPTON SHOREBREAK

Nathan Berumen directs all the dining and imbibing at the Kimpton Shorebreak Fort Lauderdale Beach Resort. "I've been in hospitality for close to twenty years now, learned my fundamentals in fast-paced bars on the West Coast while researching cocktail history, reading about Don the Beachcomber and Trader Vic, and figuring out how to craft a balanced drink," Berumen says.

As the pandemic set in, Berumen and his wife contemplated a move out of California. Texas and Australia were on the table, but they landed in Florida. In Miami, he helped open Carbone for the MFG Hospitality Group, worked at Sexy Fish as a sommelier, and tended bar, honing his style. "I wanted to bring layered cocktails with fresh ingredients and proper techniques that weren't overly sweet to Florida," he says.

A message on LinkedIn drew him just north to Fort Lauderdale. There, he was tasked with developing the bar program for Escape Rooftop Bar at the Kimpton Shorebreak. "We have a pool, but I didn't want it to be just a beach bar," he says. Where Florida's Intracoastal Waterway meets Fort Lauderdale Beach, Berumen's elevated tiki mixology has flourished.

VANILLA SYRUP: Split 2 Tahitian vanilla beans lengthwise and scrape the seeds (caviar) from the inside. In a small saucepan, combine 2 cups water and 2 cups fine sugar and bring the mixture to boil, stirring until the sugar is dissolved. Lower the heat, add the vanilla seeds and pods, cover, and simmer for 4 minutes. Remove from heat and let the syrup infuse overnight. Fine-strain.

MANGO COCKTAIL

ESCAPE ROOFTOP BAR
2900 RIOMAR STREET, FORT LAUDERDALE

Highlighting Florida ingredients is at the heart of Nathan Berumen's cocktail program at Escape Rooftop Bar. "Florida has the best mangoes in the country, and I wanted to showcase that ingredient with a cocktail that isn't your traditional Mango Margarita or Old Fashioned," Berumen says. "I chose Suntory Whisky Toki for its salinity and light floral aspects that would bring out the mango's natural sweetness while adding complexity. The dash of saline solution opens up the sour citrus in the lime juice and creates that perfect trinity of sweet, sour, and bitter."

GLASSWARE: Rocks glass

- **2 oz. Suntory Whisky Toki**
- **½ oz. mango puree**
- **½ oz. fresh lime juice**
- **¼ oz. Vanilla Syrup (see recipe at left)**
- **¼ oz. Aperol**
- **Dash Saline Solution (see recipe on page 14)**

1. Combine all of the ingredients in a cocktail shaker with ice and shake for 8 to 10 seconds.

2. Grab a rocks glass and place a big ice rock in the glass.

3. Strain the cocktail over the ice rock into the glass.

PLANE TO SIRACUSA

LA FUGA
2900 RIOMAR STREET, FORT LAUDERDALE

Nathan Berumen employed milk washing to the Plane to Siracusa, a take on the classic Paper Plane cocktail invented by Sam Ross in 2008. Also, his wife "grew up in Syracuse, Italy and I was looking to create some new Italian cocktails for La Fuga, so this is my homage to her. The Paper Plane has always been one of my go-to cocktails, and I wanted to see how I could shake it up with different measurements and a different look. Typically a brownish-reddish hue, I wanted something more attractive. Milk washing is one of the oldest tricks in the book, and the technique allowed me to create a crystal-clear cocktail. It's so beautiful, no garnish needed—express the oil from a lemon peel, and run the lemon twist around the glass rim. You get those oils on your lips, you get that first aromatic experience and the beauty in that translucent-style cocktail. It takes time, but it's worth the wait."

GLASSWARE: Rocks glass

- **1 oz. Bulleit Bourbon**
- **1 oz. Aperol**
- **1 oz. Amaro Nonino Quintessentia**
- **1 oz. fresh lemon juice**
- **8 oz. whole milk**
- **Lemon peel, to express**

1. Combine all of the ingredients, except for the milk and lemon peel, in a container. Pour the milk into a separate container.

2. Add the ingredients from the first container to the milk. It's important to do it this way, and not the other way, as it activates the "curd" process instantly. Place the container in the refrigerator for 24 hours.

3. Line a fine-mesh strainer with pre-soaked coffee filters and filter the mixture 3 times, until it is transparent.

4. Pour the clarified batch over a pre-stamped large ice cube into a rocks glass.

5. Express the lemon oils from a lemon peel over the drink, then discard the peel.

MIAMI MULE

Guava brings the Miami to this version of the Moscow Mule.

GLASSWARE: Mule cup

GARNISH: Rosemary sprig; lime peel, expressed

- 1½ oz. Tito's Handmade Vodka
- 1½ oz. Guava Rosemary Syrup (see recipe)
- 1 oz. Lillet Blanc
- ½ oz. fresh lime juice
- Ginger beer, to top

1. Combine all of the ingredients, except for the ginger beer, in a mule cup and add ice.

2. Top with ginger beer.

3. Express a lime peel over the drink then add the peel and a rosemary sprig as garnishes.

GUAVA ROSEMARY SYRUP: In a saucepan over medium-high heat, bring 500 ml water to a boil. Add 5 stems rosemary, 500 grams sugar, and 500 grams guava puree and stir until the sugar is dissolved. Remove from heat, allow the syrup to cool, and strain. Freeze for at least 4 hours before use.

THE CHAIRMAN'S COSMO

SOFF'S
19999 WEST COUNTRY CLUB DRIVE, AVENTURA

This Cosmopolitan take pays homage to Frank Sinatra's nickname, "Chairman of the Board."

GLASSWARE: Martini glass

GARNISH: Lemon twist

- 1½ oz. vodka
- ½ oz. Cointreau
- ½ oz. cranberry juice
- ½ oz. fresh lime juice

1. Combine all of the ingredients in a martini glass and stir gently.

2. Garnish with a lemon twist.

SPICY AVOCADO MARGARITA

LONA COCINA & TEQUILERIA
321 NORTH FORT LAUDERDALE BEACH BOULEVARD, FORT LAUDERDALE

This Spicy Margarita gets a hit of pureed avocado to complement any tasty taco on your menu.

GLASSWARE: Margarita glass

GARNISH: Jalapeño slice

- 2 oz. Ghost Blanco Tequila
- ½ oz. fresh lime juice
- ½ oz. agave nectar
- 1 tablespoon avocado puree

1. Combine all of the ingredients in a cocktail shaker with ice and shake well.
2. Strain the cocktail over ice into a margarita glass.
3. Garnish with jalapeño slice.

PASION PICANTE

LONA COCINA & TEQUILERIA
321 NORTH FORT LAUDERDALE BEACH BOULEVARD,
FORT LAUDERDALE

Morita chiles are a mainstay in Latin cuisine, and the syrup in this recipe is easy to make. If you can't find moritas, substitute dried chipotle peppers.

GLASSWARE: Collins glass

GARNISH: Sliced peppers

- Tajín, for the rim
- 1 oz. Hiatus Tequila Blanco
- 1 oz. 400 Conejos Espadín Joven Mezcal
- 1 oz. Cointreau
- 1 oz. passion fruit juice
- 1 oz. Morita Chile Syrup (see recipe)

1. Wet the rim of a collins glass then dip the glass in Tajín to give it a rim.

2. Combine all of the ingredients in a cocktail shaker with ice and shake well.

3. Strain the cocktail over fresh ice into the rimmed collins glass.

4. Garnish with sliced peppers.

MORITA CHILE SYRUP: In a saucepan over medium heat, combine 1 quart simple syrup and 2 cinnamon sticks. Break up 5 dried morita chiles and add them to syrup. Simmer for 10 minutes then allow the syrup to cool. Strain and refrigerate.

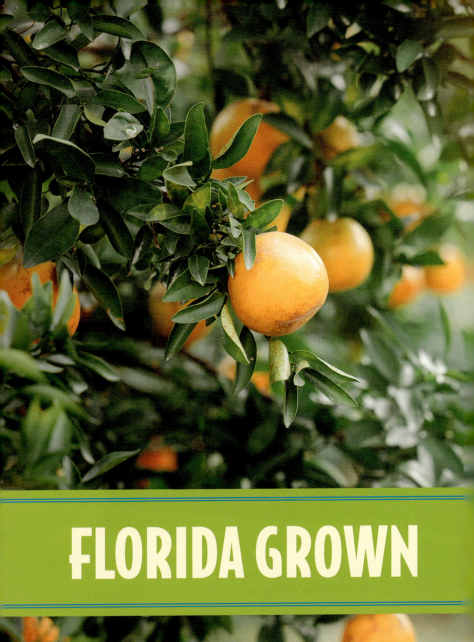

FLORIDA GROWN

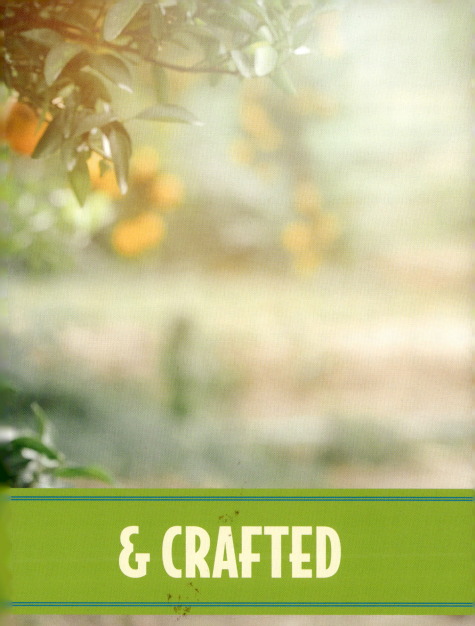

& CRAFTED

The Sunshine State bursts with a kaleidoscope of produce that inspires bartenders from urban cities to small towns. In St. Augustine, they lean into their Minorcan heritage with the datil pepper. It flourishes only in this pocket of the country and adds a spicy-sweet profile to cocktails. South Florida has all the tropical fruit: mangoes, papaya, dragonfruit, loquats, and more add that taste of the islands to any concoction. Mint blankets gardens across the state, and basil prolifically multiplies in any patch of earth it is planted in. Wildflower and Tupelo honey harvested at apiaries around the state provide native sweeteners. Of course, citrus is king—Florida boasts groves of oranges, grapefruit, and the backbone of any bar, lemons and limes. To promote Florida's agricultural abundance in the cocktails space, tasting rooms at distilleries around the state have become classrooms for the curious and showcases for local produce farmers and small-batch makers, representing the best of Florida with every crop, blend, and bottle.

HARRISON HOLDITCH AND DAVID KAPITANOFF, DISTILLERY 98

Harrison Holditch's brewing career started in college but it wasn't until 2019 that he and his brother-in-law, David Kapitanoff, realized their dream of opening a distillery. Distillery 98 in Santa Rosa Beach is where they craft their vodka with 100% non-GMO Florida Panhandle ingredients, utilizing a unique filtration process with Gulf Coast oyster shells.

"It's smooth. It kind of releases from your palate because we take some of those fumes out, and you get some sweetness—earth tones from corn that was in the ground six months ago," says Holditch.

In keeping with their commitment to sustainability, they donate the leftover mash corn to a livestock farm in Holmes County and pay attention to water waste. "We have a shallow well to bring in natural groundwater. Once all of our equipment has cooled, we recycle all the water back into the ground. We are 100% zero-waste," says Holditch.

They became the first distillery to use a cardboard spirit bottle in 2022. The Half Shell Vodka packaging has six times less carbon footprint than the typical glass bottle that most distilleries use. It's crafted from 97% recycled cardboard, making it convenient to tote to the beach, on a boat, by the pool, or anywhere you want to sip on a fresh cocktail.

"We camp, hunt, and think about conservation. We've been taught since we were little that you pack out what you pack in; you don't overuse your resources," Holditch said. "We carried that with us as we set up the distillery and moved to this type of bottle."

They just released their first whiskey, and on the horizon are a couple of flavored vodkas, a gin crafted with Florida botanicals, and a Florida cane sugar–based rum. "We have all these amazing ingredients at our fingertips, whether it's wild rosemary growing in the state parks, the Tupelo honey, kumquats, or the sweet watermelon. We're planting lemongrass and a few other things at the distillery to use in our coming gin. We're proud to use local resources—it makes our spirits original, and you can taste the true flavors of our area in every pour."

LOTUS DROP

DISTILLERY 98
835 SERENOA ROAD, SANTA ROSA BEACH

If you found yourself enmeshed in the drama of the show *White Lotus*, this namesake drink offers a little coastal flair.

GLASSWARE: Rocks glass

GARNISH: Lime wedge

- **2 oz. Cucumber-Infused Vodka (see recipe)**
- **1 oz. Coconut Syrup (see recipe)**
- **½ oz. fresh lime juice**

1. Fill a cocktail shaker with ice. Combine all of the ingredients in the shaker and shake until well chilled, about 15 to 20 seconds.

2. Fill a rocks glass with fresh ice. Strain the cocktail into the rocks glass and garnish with a lime wedge on the rim of the glass.

CUCUMBER-INFUSED VODKA: Wash and slice a cucumber. Place the cucumber slices in a jar, then pour 1 (750 ml) bottle of Distillery 98 Half Shell Vodka over them, and seal the jar. Store it in a cool, dark place for 3 to 5 days, then strain and rebottle.

COCONUT SYRUP: In a saucepan over low heat, combine 1 cup coconut milk and 1 cup sugar, stirring until the sugar dissolves completely. Let the mixture simmer gently for a few minutes, then remove from heat and let the syrup cool. Store it in an airtight container and refrigerate for up to 2 weeks.

184 — FLORIDA COCKTAILS

KAP'S REVENGE

DISTILLERY 98
835 SERENOA ROAD, SANTA ROSA BEACH

Inspired by Snoop Dogg's Olympic torch–bearing appearance, Kap's Revenge brings together strong, spicy, fun flavors. If you want it extra spicy, like his dancing alongside the U.S. women's gymnastics team, muddle some fresh jalapeños in the mix.

GLASSWARE: Rocks glass

GARNISH: Lime wedge

- 2 oz. Jalapeño-Infused Vodka (see recipe)
- ¼ oz. fresh lime juice
- Grapefruit juice, to top

1. Fill a rocks glass with fresh ice. Pour the vodka and lime juice into the glass and top with grapefruit juice, filling to the top.
2. Stir gently to mix the ingredients.
3. Garnish with a fresh lime wedge on the rim of the glass.

JALAPEÑO-INFUSED VODKA: Slice 2 to 3 jalapeños, removing the seeds for less heat or keeping them, depending on the preferred heat level. Place the jalapeño slices in a jar and pour 1 (750 ml) bottle of Distillery 98 Half Shell Vodka over them. Seal the jar. Let it sit for 1 to 2 days in a cool, dark place, shaking occasionally. Taste periodically until the desired heat level is reached, then strain and rebottle.

VELVET BUZZ

The first sip of the Velvet Buzz brings shades of a classic Lemon Drop with the addition of floral lavender notes and fresh lime. The kicker, though, is the smoky rosemary that hits your nose before it even hits your tastebuds—it brings a woodiness that recalls the tall pine trees surrounding the distillery.

GLASSWARE: Collins glass

GARNISH: Lightly torched rosemary sprig, dehydrated lime wheel

- 2 oz. Distillery 98 Half Shell Vodka
- 1 oz. Lavender Syrup (see recipe)
- ½ oz. fresh lime juice

1. Fill a collins glass with fresh ice. Combine the ingredients in a cocktail shaker with ice and shake until well chilled.
2. Strain the cocktail into the collins glass over the ice.
3. Lightly torch a rosemary sprig and carefully place it on top of the drink to garnish, along with a dehydrated lime wheel.

LAVENDER SYRUP: In a saucepan over medium-low heat, combine 1 cup water, 1 cup sugar, and 1 tablespoon dried culinary lavender and bring the mixture to a simmer, stirring until the sugar dissolves. Remove from heat and let the syrup steep for 15 to 20 minutes. Strain, cool, and store in an airtight container in the refrigerator for up to 2 weeks.

GOLD RUSH

DISTILLERY 98
835 SERENOA ROAD, SANTA ROSA BEACH

The classic bourbon, lemon, and honey syrup cocktail invented at Milk & Honey in 2001 gets a revamp at Distillery 98, where they sub the bourbon for their vodka, infused with local honey.

GLASSWARE: Rocks glass

GARNISH: Rosemary sprig, honeycomb

- **2 oz. Honey-Infused Vodka (see recipe)**
- **½ oz. fresh lemon juice**
- **½ oz. Rosemary Syrup (see recipe)**
- **Soda water, to top**

1. Fill a rocks glass with fresh ice. Combine all of the ingredients, except for the soda water, In a cocktail shaker with ice and shake until well chilled.

2. Strain the cocktail into the rocks glass over the ice and top with soda water. Give the drink a gentle stir to combine.

3. Garnish with a rosemary sprig and a piece of honeycomb.

HONEY-INFUSED VODKA: In a saucepan over low heat, warm honey, to taste, slightly until it becomes more liquid. Pour the warm honey into a jar, then add 1 (750 ml) bottle of Distillery 98 Half Shell Vodka. Seal the jar. Shake well to mix, then let it sit in a cool, dark place for 1 to 2 days, shaking occasionally. Strain if needed.

ROSEMARY SYRUP: In a saucepan over medium-low heat, combine 1 cup water, 1 cup sugar, and 3 to 4 sprigs of fresh rosemary and bring the mixture to a simmer, stirring until the sugar dissolves. Remove from heat and let the syrup steep for 20 to 30 minutes. Strain, cool, and store in an airtight container in the refrigerator for up to 2 weeks.

FESTIVAL SPOTLIGHT: CRAFTED IN ALYS BEACH

The white-washed Mediterranean walls of Alys Beach serve as the backdrop for a gathering of small-batch producers, makers, and distillers, where a slew of events showcase the finer points of mixology. It starts with an evening with Emerald Coast Storytellers sharing stories around a fire. Friday brings Firkin Fête, where the brewers tap firkins they have developed in the same method they made beer back in the fifteenth century.

Throughout the weekend, experiential mixology dinners and seminars pop up all over the coastal beach town. A holiday makers market offers a chance to interact with local artisans, take a class, and squirrel away some unique holiday gifts. Pickleball & Picklebacks joins the lineup in 2024 as the culminating event, but the Spirited Soirée on Saturday should not be missed—it is a stroll through the winding streets and parks as celebrated bartenders, bars, and restaurants mix up their signature cocktails and snacks.

FLORIDA DISTILLERIES

When building your home bar, check out these distilleries that lean on Florida ingredients and heritage.

ST. AUGUSTINE DISTILLERY
112 RIBERIA STREET, ST. AUGUSTINE

Located in the bottom floor of a historic ice plant, in the first freed African American neighborhood in the United States, this distillery has stories to tell. Not only did they craft the first Florida bourbon, but all of their spirits have devoted fans among the bar industry. Their vodka uses a Florida sugarcane base and their gin features three types of Florida citrus. But the real narrative here is their commitment to sustainability—they employ an innovative water reuse program, they spent years painstakingly restoring an abandoned ice plant, making sure to keep it as authentic as possible, and they pour money into their surrounding community through Habitat for Humanity builds, support for the arts, and limiting their carbon footprint by collaborating with a local winery for their port-finishing barrels. They won the American Distilling Institute's Distillery of the Year award in 2024. If you are in St. Augustine, they have tours, tastings, cocktail classes, and even a Certified Bourbon Steward course in conjunction with the Stave and Thief Society in Louisville.

Manifest Distilling

Hemingway Distillery

MANIFEST DISTILLING
960 EAST FORSYTH STREET, JACKSONVILLE

American-made distillation equipment and grains sourced from a network of co-ops throughout North America are the bones of this distillery's story. They are a certified organic facility, supporting their commitment to foster sustainable agricultural practices, and they incorporate many Florida ingredients into their spirits. Their portfolio includes Florida Citrus Vodka (Florida-grown oranges, grapefruit, and lemons), Florida Botanical Gin (highlights a delicate balance of botanicals that can all be found growing here), and the first-ever Florida-produced Fernet, Fernet Manifesto. It's a rich, complex, sippable version of the herbal liqueur. They also have a cocktail room where fresh herbs and citrus line the bar, ready for the next drink.

HEMINGWAY DISTILLERY
201 SIMONTON STREET, KEY WEST

Papa Hemingway had many passions, and he wrang every second out of life, but one of his greatest loves was his boat. This rum captures that spirit of adventure and is underpinned by a commitment to conservation—CEO Steve Groth collaborated with the Hemingway family to build a brand that carries on Papa's legacy and work as a conservationist. Most proceeds from the rum goes to protecting and restoring oceans and coastal environments (like Key West) in places where Hemingway once lived. Master distiller Ron Call hand-selects rums from Barbados, the Dominican Republic, Panama, Venezuela, and Key West, then blends them into the selection available at Hemingway. Sloppy Joe's, Hemingway's favorite haunt in Key West, uses many of their rums in their signature cocktails.

CHAINBRIDGE DISTILLERY
3500 NE 11TH AVENUE, OAKLAND PARK

This family-owned and operated distillery leans on their wine-making background from the Tokaj region of the northeastern border of Hungary and Slovakia. Along with wine, the family brought their "Pálinka" eau de vie–style fruit brandy to Florida. Each piece of fruit is hand-selected and each batch of brandy rests for at least three months before filtering and bottling. They also craft Florida Basil Vodka, employing a sugarcane base and flavored with two different varieties of basil grown on Sunshine State farms, and Nikhil Abuvala, owner of Daytrader Tiki, loves their Florida-barreled gin.

GASPARILLA DISTILLERY
2102 EAST 4TH AVENUE, TAMPA

Located in Historic Ybor City in Tampa, this pirate-inspired distillery embraces the lore of Captain José Gaspar and his marauding pirate crew—some say you can feel their ghosts touring the facility. The distillery utilizes top-grade molasses from Okeelanta Sugar Mills in South Florida to ferment their rum for seven days. Their Gasparilla Reserve won the 2020 Best of Class Craft Rum for Florida in the American Distillers Institute competition. Every spirit is distilled, aged, blended, and infused in-house from scratch. They also make vodka and fruit brandy, but rum is their specialty. Tampa's love of pirate José Gaspar runs so deep that they hold the annual Gasparilla celebration in his honor every January. Stop by, grab some grog, and enjoy the spectacle of over 750 swashbucklers invading Tampa Bay.

NATALIE'S ORCHID ISLAND JUICE

As I traveled around Florida checking out bars, I noticed an ingredient in coolers across the state: Natalie's juices, usually lemon, lime, or orange juice. When I asked bartenders about why they chose this brand, the answer remained the same: the only ingredient is the juice of the fruit. Natalie's has taken the work out of hand-squeezing all that citrus needed to supply the bar.

Back on Thanksgiving of 1989, Marygrace Sexton started Natalie's Orchid Island Juice Company after pulling her daughter Natalie around the family orchards, dreaming of fresh-squeezed juice. Bobby Sexton, her husband, was a fourth-generation Florida citrus grower producing what Marygrace knew were the best oranges around. That fledgling business blossomed into a women-owned operation that produces simple juices with no preservatives, no artificial ingredients, no GMOs, and minimal processing, sold in over 32 states and 50 countries. But they still source from local Florida and regional farmers, where fruit is hand-selected and handcrafted in small batches.

"Natalie's ethos and foundation is rooted in a commitment to support Florida's rich citrus heritage. I founded Natalie's with a purpose-driven passion: to honor the legacy of Florida's generational citrus farming community by producing juice that is as pure as the fruit itself," Marygrace Sexton, CEO and founder of Natalie's Orchid Island Juice Company, says.

D. RODRIGUEZ OVERPROOF DAIQUIRI

ST. AUGUSTINE DISTILLERY
112 RIBERIA STREET, ST. AUGUSTINE

Named for Danny Rodriguez, the first employee at the distillery, the label on the rum features five blue stars representing Rodriguez's Honduran heritage.

GLASSWARE: Coupe glass
GARNISH: Lime wheel

- 2 oz. D. Rodriguez & Sons Overproof Rum
- 1 oz. fresh lime juice
- ½ oz. simple syrup

1. Combine all of the ingredients in a cocktail shaker with ice and shake until the ice cracks.
2. Strain the cocktail into a coupe glass and garnish with a lime wheel.

TOASTED SUNSET COCKTAIL

ST. AUGUSTINE DISTILLERY
112 RIBERIA STREET, ST. AUGUSTINE

Datil peppers lend kick to this cocktail, crafted with a Florida bourbon finished in lightly toasted American oak.

GLASSWARE: Collins glass

GARNISH: Lemon peel on a skewer

- ½ oz. cherry juice
- ½ oz. Datil Pepper Honey (see recipe)
- 2 oz. St. Augustine Distillery Florida Straight Bourbon
- ¾ oz. fresh lemon juice
- 2 dashes Angostura bitters
- 4 oz. seltzer water

1. Combine the datil pepper honey and cherry juice in a small bowl and set it aside.

2. Combine the remaining ingredients in a mixing glass with ice and stir for 10 to 15 seconds.

3. Strain the cocktail into a collins glass over ice. Top with the cherry-pepper honey syrup for a layered effect.

4. Garnish with a skewered lemon peel.

DATIL PEPPER HONEY: Add 3 datil peppers, sliced, to a clean jar. Pour honey, as needed, over the pepper slices. Cover the jar and refrigerate it overnight (or less time, for less spice). Strain.

POT OF GOLD

ST. AUGUSTINE DISTILLERY
112 RIBERIA STREET, ST. AUGUSTINE

This bourbon-based concoction draws balance from two sources of sweet plus the tartness of lime juice. The Pot of Gold is meant to be a St. Patrick's Day libation.

GLASSWARE: Coupe glass

GARNISH: Lime wheel

- **2 oz. St. Augustine Distillery Florida Straight Bourbon**
- **¾ oz. fresh lime juice**
- **¾ oz. simple syrup**
- **2 Yes Cocktail Co. Elderflower Bitters Infused Cocktail Cubes**

1. Combine all of the ingredients in a cocktail shaker.

2. Muddle the cocktail cubes until they are fully broken down.

3. Add ice and shake until well combined.

4. Strain the cocktail into a coupe glass and garnish with a lime wheel.

STRAWBERRY BASIL BOURBON SMASH

ST. AUGUSTINE DISTILLERY
112 RIBERIA STREET, ST. AUGUSTINE

A classic Smash cocktail always uses crushed or pebble ice to keep the drink cooler over time. The pairing of basil and strawberry comes together with lemon juice, simple syrup, and soda water to highlight the Florida-crafted bourbon.

GLASSWARE: Highball glass

GARNISH: Basil sprig, strawberry slice

- 3 strawberries
- 3 basil leaves
- ½ oz. fresh lemon juice
- ¾ oz. Simple Syrup (see recipe on page 14)

- 2 oz. St. Augustine Distillery Florida Straight Bourbon
- Soda water, to top

1. In a highball glass, muddle the strawberries.
2. Slap the basil leaves between your hands to release the flavor oils, and add them to the glass.
3. Add the lemon juice, simple syrup, and bourbon. Fill the glass with crushed ice and top with soda water.
4. Stir to combine and garnish with fresh basil sprig and a sliced strawberry.

DAVID ROTH AND JACOB LESITSKY, TSUNAMI

Walking into Tsunami in Lakewood Ranch outside of Sarasota, you don't expect to see a cocktail legend behind the bar, but you do: David Roth, an industry veteran of over thirty years.

In 1992, a few rounds of foosball ignited his career in bartending. After winning numerous awards for his cocktail creations, in 2020 as bars closed, he moved to Florida. A mentee of Naren Young and Luis Hernandez, Roth develops recipes that satisfy the two tenets Young taught him: make it fun and make it delicious.

Roth has three rules behind the bar:

1. Be on time.
2. Be present.
3. Play through the whistle.

Roth recruited Jacob Lesitsky, the 2022 Woodford Reserve Manhattan Experience Tampa winner and another Florida transplant.

David Roth

Lesitsky knows the business through and through. "Even though there are only thirty covers on the books, the party bus is right around the corner," he says. "Be prepared to get your ass handed to you. I'm not a big sports guy, but the analogy makes sense. Even after the rush, when you start to slow down, your guests at the bar still matter. We're fighting for seconds—when it's slower, maybe putting a drink out in five minutes isn't that big of a deal, but when we're in the weeds, that five-minute drink can turn into ten or fifteen minutes. You need to get that drink out, make sure it hits the table fresh, the ice looks good, and the garnish is done correctly—it's the little details."

To that end, Roth and Lesitsky batch cocktails as much as possible, except for citrus. If they can turn a five-touch drink into a two-touch drink, they succeed in the fight for seconds. Roth keeps an inventive menu at Tsunami with riffs on Sours, Martinis, and Daiquiris, but the real magic is their secret menu, a collection of their award-winning drinks not on regular rotation, but iykyk.

Jacob Lesitsky

BLUEBERRY CHEONG: In an airtight container or resealable bag, combine 1 pound fresh Florida blueberries, washed and dried, and 1 pound superfine (caster) sugar. Mash the blueberries slightly. Store the container in a cool, dark place for a week, checking daily to see if there's any gas buildup. Burp the bag, or carefully let the gas out of the container, and reseal. Once the sugar has fully dissolved and drawn all the blueberry juice out, strain and bottle the cheong. Label and date.

A GIFT HORSE

Inspired by a recipe for Blueberry and Horseradish Jam in the cookbook *The Flavor Matrix* by Pensacola chef James Briscione, this Sour taps into David Roth's love of unusual flavor pairings. "A Gift Horse is just fun and delicious," Roth says. "I like to make a Korean-style syrup called *cheong* with fresh Florida blueberries, but a commercial syrup from Reàl or Monin would work as well. The color is super dark and it leans on local produce, which I love. It's my new up-and-coming drink." Guests in the know at Tsunami will recognize this as one of Roth's most popular secret drinks.

GLASSWARE: Double rocks glass

GARNISH: Lemon peel, expressed

- 1 oz. London dry gin
- 1 oz. blanco tequila
- ¾ oz. Blueberry Cheong (see recipe)
- ¾ oz. fresh lemon juice
- ½ barspoon Kelchner's Horse-Radish

1. Combine all of the ingredients in a shaker tin and shake with ice until very cold, 15 to 20 seconds.
2. Double-strain the cocktail into a double rocks glass and add ice.
3. Express a lemon peel over the top and add the peel as a garnish.

THE FANTASTIC VOYAGE

TSUNAMI
11627 STATE ROAD 70 E, LAKEWOOD RANCH

Jacob Lesitsky took second place at the Jefferson's Old Fashioned Cocktail Competition in 2023. Wanting to create something with local ingredients, he asked the chef at Kojo to save the destined-to-be-discarded oyster shells after dinner service prepping was completed for a unique infusion that has a briny, umami flavor that makes the cocktail pop.

GLASSWARE: Double rocks glass

GARNISH: Nori square, Laphroaig 10 spritz, Yuzu Furikake Sand (see recipe), caviar spoon on the side

- 2 oz. Gulf Oyster Shell–Infused Bourbon (see recipe)
- ¼ oz. Dashi Syrup (see recipe)
- 2 dashes The Japanese Bitters Yuzu Bitters
- 8 drops 20% MSG Saline Solution (see recipe)

1. Combine all of the ingredients in a mixing glass with ice and stir for 20 to 30 seconds.
2. Strain the cocktail into a large rocks glass over a large ice cube.
3. To garnish, place a nori square on top of the cube, then spritz the glass with scotch out of an atomizer. Then place some Yuzu Furikake sand and a caviar spoon on the side as an accompaniment.

GULF OYSTER SHELL–INFUSED BOURBON: Scrub Gulf oyster shells, as needed, then combine them with Jefferson's Ocean Bourbon in a container. Let the oysters infuse the bourbon for 72 hours. Remove and discard the shells, then strain the bourbon through a coffee filter–lined chinois and rebottle it.

DASHI SYRUP: Combine 500 ml Dashi Stock (see recipe) and 1 kilogram white sugar in a large container and blend on high for 2 minutes. Let the mixture settle for 5 minutes, then blend for 2 minutes. Let the mixture settle for 5 minutes more and blend one final time for 2 minutes.

DASHI STOCK: In a saucepan over low heat, combine 32 oz. cold water and 14 grams kombu and bring to a simmer. Turn off the heat, cover the pot, and let the mixture steep for 30 minutes. Remove the kombu from pot with a slotted spoon and return the liquid to a simmer. Add 50 grams bonito flakes, turn off the heat, cover the pot, and let the stock steep for 30 minutes. Strain the stock through a chinois and store in the refrigerator up to 1 week.

20% MSG SALINE SOLUTION: Combine 40 grams MSG and 200 ml water in a large container and blend until the MSG is dissolved. Store indefinitely at room temperature.

YUZU FURIKAKE SAND: Run yuzu furikake through a spice grinder until it reaches a sandy consistency. Return the sand to its original packaging for storage.

ACROSS THE YUZUVERSE

Jacob Lesitsky serves this one at Tsunami without the strawberry glitter garnish, but if you ask him nicely, he might bring it out. Across the Yuzuverse won Best Vodka Cocktail in the 2024 Sarasota-Manatee Originals Set the Bar Competition. Lesitsky cautions to be sure to get a salt-free yuzu juice to maintain the integrity of the drink's flavor.

GLASSWARE: Nick & Nora glass

- Rosewater, for spritzing
- Strawberry Glitter (see recipe)
- 2 oz. vodka
- ¾ oz. yuzu juice
- ¾ oz. Strawberry-Vanilla Syrup (see recipe)

1. Spritz the entire outside of a Nick & Nora glass with rosewater from an atomizer, then dip the glass in Strawberry Glitter until it is completely coated. Place the coated glass in the freezer.
2. Combine the remaining ingredients in a cocktail shaker with ice and shake for 10 seconds. Take the chilled Nick & Nora out of the freezer.
3. Double-strain the cocktail into the chilled Nick & Nora.

STRAWBERRY-VANILLA SYRUP: Combine 1 liter Heavy Vanilla Syrup (see recipe) and 1 liter Strawberry Reàl in a container and stir to combine.

HEAVY VANILLA SYRUP: Split and scrape 2 to 3 vanilla beans. Combine 1 liter water, 2 kilograms sugar, and the scraped vanilla beans in a container, reserving the vanilla pods for later, and blend on high for 5 minutes. Let the mixture settle for 5 minutes, then blend for 2 additional minutes. Add the vanilla bean pods to the syrup. Store in the refrigerator for up to 3 weeks.

STRAWBERRY GLITTER: Sift 50 grams freeze-dried strawberry powder into a container. Add 150 grams white sanding sugar, 75 grams Maldon Sea Salt Flakes, 2.5 grams white luster dust, and 300 milligrams edible gold flakes, seal the container, and shake to combine.

LAVA LAMP

TSUNAMI
11627 STATE ROAD 70 E, LAKEWOOD RANCH

Bartender David Roth entered the Lava Lamp, his take on a Tequila Sunrise, into the first Don Julio StarBack Finals in 2019 and won. "The prize was working the 2020 Oscars in Los Angeles with Charles Joly and Liquid Pro. It was an incredible experience. A bucket list item to be sure," Roth says. Next time you visit him at Tsunami, ask him to make you one.

GLASSWARE: Coupe glass
GARNISH: Avocado oil drops

- **3 to 4 sage leaves**
- **1½ oz. blanco tequila**
- **1½ oz. fresh Florida orange juice**
- **½ oz. agave nectar**
- **½ oz. fresh Florida lime juice**
- **Avocado oil in an eye dropper**

1. Chill a coupe glass. Roll and press the sage leaves in your hands to release their oils, then place the leaves in a shaker tin.
2. Add the remaining ingredients with ice and shake until very cold, 15 to 20 seconds.
3. Double-strain the cocktail into the chilled coupe.
4. Using an eye dropper, dot the surface of the cocktail with avocado oil.

BAY GOT ME SIPPIN'

Ingi Sigurdsson, a seasoned cocktail craftsman with a twenty-year career in the food and beverage industry and currently the beverage director for Haute Hospitality in St. Petersburg, oversees the bar programs for Allelo, Juno & The Peacock, and Pluma Lounge. For Allelo, he wanted to create a cocktail with bay leaf as one of the main flavors. He experimented with the bay leaves, trying to find a way to make them shine, eventually settling on blending them into a syrup. "This process resulted in an incredible color for the final cocktail. Green is often a challenging color to achieve naturally in cocktails, but this syrup retains its vibrant hue and bright vegetal notes for about two weeks," he says. He added vanilla to complement the fresh bay leaves, subtle vanilla notes. "The vegetal flavors pair beautifully with tequila, and I added a touch of elderflower, mezcal, and mango for added complexity."

GLASSWARE: Rocks glass

GARNISH: Fresh bay leaf

- 1½ oz. tequila
- ¾ oz. Bay Leaf Syrup (see récipe)
- ¾ oz. fresh lime juice
- ½ oz. mezcal
- ¼ oz. elderflower liqueur
- ¼ oz. Thatcher's Organic Mango Liqueur

1. Combine all of the ingredients in a shaking tin with ice and shake.
2. Strain the cocktail over fresh ice into a rocks glass and garnish with a bay leaf.

BAY LEAF SYRUP: Add 5 oz. white sugar, ⅓ oz. vanilla extract, 1 teaspoon kosher salt, and 5 oz. water to a blender. While blending, gradually add 1 oz. bay leaves, about a quarter at a time, to ensure everything combines and mixes properly. Once fully combined, blend on high for 1 minute. Strain the syrup through a fine-mesh strainer.

OLIVE OIL SYRUP: In a saucepan over medium-high heat, combine 7 oz. water, 2.7 grams gum arabic, and 0.3 grams xanthan gum and stick blend. Bring the mixture to a boil. Turn off the heat and transfer the mixture to a new container. Using a stick blender, slowly drizzle in 130 grams hot pepper–infused olive oil, ensuring you go slowly to emulsify the oil into the water. Add 7 oz. sugar and whisk until the sugar is dissolved.

LIKE A VIRGIN

Beverage director Ingi Sigurdsson highlights the importance of olive oil in the Mediterranean by incorporating it into cocktails for Allelo, a Mediterranean and Aegean restaurant. "The extra viscosity from the emulsified olive oil syrup made the cocktail taste a bit too hot, as the drink lingers on the tongue. To achieve the proper balance, we add ½ oz. of water to the recipe," he says.

GLASSWARE: Coupe glass

GARNISH: Parsley oil droplets, red paprika oil droplets

- 1 oz. Fords London Dry Gin
- ¾ oz. fresh lime juice
- ½ oz. Olive Oil Syrup (see recipe)
- ½ oz. Dolin Génépy le Chamois Liqueur
- ½ oz. mastiha
- ½ oz. Pierre Ferrand Dry Curaçao
- Dash St. George Absinthe Verte

1. Combine all of the ingredients in a shaking tin with ice and shake.

2. Strain the cocktail into a coupe.

3. Garnish with a few droplets of parsley oil and red paprika olive oil.

DIP BABY DIP

S arah Snyder began developing her own cocktail recipes while managing an award-winning agave bar in Buffalo. In 2024, she relocated to St. Petersburg and helped launch Pluma Lounge. Inspired by the complexity of mole negro and its roots in Oaxaca, Snyder developed this cocktail for the opening menu. "Highlighted by smoky and bitter notes, it drinks like a Negroni or Boulevardier, with intricate layers of rich, deep flavors," she says.

GLASSWARE: Rocks glass

GARNISH: Mole Tootsie Roll (see recipe) on a skewer

- 1 oz. Monkey Shoulder
- ½ oz. Balcones Brimstone
- ½ oz. Giffard Crème de Cacao
- ½ oz. Cynar 70 Proof
- ¼ oz. Boyd & Blair Ancho Chili Liqueur
- ¼ oz. Luxardo Amaro Abano
- ¼ oz. Vedrenne Liqueur de Banane
- Orange peel, to express

1. Combine all of the ingredients, except for the orange peel, in a mixing glass with ice and stir.
2. Strain the cocktail into a rocks glass over a large ice cube. Express an orange peel over the drink and discard.
3. Garnish with a Mole Tootsie Roll.

MOLE TOOTSIE ROLL: Place 50 grams melted cocoa butter, 120 grams cocoa powder, 210 grams powdered sugar, 125 grams dry milk powder, 1 cup corn syrup, and 65 grams Marina Mole, oil discarded, into a KitchenAid mixer. Use the dough hook attachment to mix until very well combined, or mix and knead by hand as you would when making pasta. Portion the mixture into the size and shape of Tootsie Rolls, then wrap the portions in a candy wrapper.

JON MATEER, TPC SAWGRASS

Jon Mateer, beverage director for TPC Sawgrass, never planned to become a bartender. While pursuing a master's degree in Latin American studies in Gainesville, Mateer worked in bars. The experience of crafting cocktails and working in hospitality helped Mateer choose a different path in life.

He moved on to cocktail bars, where a manager gave him *Death & Co: Modern Classic Cocktails*, and after three years working at Death & Co. in Denver, he returned to Florida, where he found his home at one of the world's top golf courses. At Sawgrass, "there's full creative freedom, which is really exciting," he says. "The sky's the limit, but working with local ingredients provides a fresh and nuanced approach towards creating signature cocktails and places emphasis on where we all come from."

In 2022, he claimed the U.S. National Champion of the Giffard West Cup title and in 2024 was named a Top 10 US Bartender in the USBG Presents World Class Sponsored by DIAGEO competition. Never one to take himself too seriously, Mateer started a podcast called Bardtenders, where he and a group of fellow bartenders play Dungeons & Dragons while educating listeners about their industry and advocating for mental and physical wellness behind the bar. "Bartending isn't just a job," he says. "It's a lifestyle full of adventure and amazing opportunities."

THE SAWGRASS SPLASH

TPC SAWGRASS
110 CHAMPIONSHIP WAY, PONTE VEDRA BEACH

In 1982, the "Sawgrass Splash" was heard around the golfing world. Golfer Jerry Pate celebrated his TPC Sawgrass victory by pushing two golf officials into the lake at the eighteenth hole before diving in himself. "Everybody's eyes were on this inaugural event, on this monstrous green," Jon Mateer, beverage director, says, "and then something absolutely crazy and spontaneous and amazing happens. This cocktail commemorates that moment." Essentially a riff on a Screwdriver, Mateer uses fresh Florida oranges. "This cocktail is perfect for a hot day on a golf course. It's light, refreshing, and reminds you of the legacy that TPC Sawgrass has in the world of golf," he says.

GLASSWARE: Collins glass

GARNISH: Orange half-moon

- 2 oz. orange juice
- 1¼ oz. lemonade
- 1 oz. Tito's Handmade Vodka
- ½ oz. triple sec
- ¼ oz. lime juice

1. Combine all of the ingredients in a cocktail shaker with ice and shake.
2. Pour the cocktail over ice into a collins glass.
3. Garnish with an orange half moon.

THE GOLD STANDARD

TPC SAWGRASS
110 CHAMPIONSHIP WAY, PONTE VEDRA BEACH

The cocktail known as the Transfusion served as beverage director Jon Mateer's inspiration for this concoction. He swapped out the traditional grape juice for white grape juice, then added gold flakes and carbonated grapes that fizz in your mouth.

GLASSWARE: Collins glass

GARNISH: 3 Carbonated Grapes (see recipe)

- **2 oz. Gold Foil–Infused Vodka (see recipe)**
- **1 oz. white grape juice**
- **¼ oz. fresh lime juice**
- **2 oz. ginger ale, to top**

1. Combine all of the ingredients, except for the ginger ale, in a cocktail shaker with ice and shake.

2. Strain the cocktail over ice into a collins glass. Top with the ginger ale, and garnish with the Carbonated Grapes.

CARBONATED GRAPES: Fill a Cornelius keg halfway with white grapes. Connect the CO_2 line to the tank and turn on the CO_2. Keep the entire keg refrigerated overnight while still connected to the CO_2. The next day, remove the grapes from the keg.

GOLD FOIL–INFUSED VODKA: Pour 1 (5-gram) container of gold foil into 1 (1 liter) bottle of Tito's Handmade Vodka and shake until combined.

THE GRAZING GOAT

Goats were the original groundskeepers at TPC Sawgrass. Beverage director Jon Mateer took that historical tidbit and turned it into a cocktail for THE PLAYERS Championship VIP Experience. Knowing cilantro can be a little earthy, he paired it with matcha for the syrup. "For the garnish, I wanted something fun that nodded at the goats, so we took a banana leaf and trimmed it to look like fresh-cut grass," he says. "It is so refreshing after a long day on the golf course."

GLASSWARE: Rocks glass

GARNISH: Banana leaf, cut to resemble a grass blade

- Tajín, for the rim
- 1½ oz. Avocado Oil Fat-Washed Tequila (see recipe)
- ½ oz. Clément Créole Shrubb Orange Liqueur
- ½ oz. Matcha & Cilantro Syrup (see recipe)
- ½ oz. fresh lime juice

1. Wet the rim of a rocks glass with lime juice then dip the rim in Tajín to give the glass a rim.
2. Combine the remaining ingredients in a cocktail shaker with ice and shake until diluted.
3. Double-strain the cocktail over a large cube into the rimmed glass.
4. Garnish with a trimmed banana leaf.

AVOCADO OIL FAT-WASHED TEQUILA: In a Cambro or other container, combine 1 (750 ml) bottle of Maestro Dobel Diamante Tequila and 120 grams avocado oil and whisk quickly for 30 seconds. Seal and let the infusion sit at room temperature for 2 hours. Place the container in the freezer overnight, or 12 hours. Remove the container and then skim the frozen fat content from the top of the liquid. Strain the tequila through a nut bag or fine-mesh strainer.

MATCHA & CILANTRO SYRUP: Combine 1 kilogram syrup, 4 grams matcha powder, and 30 grams cilantro in a blender and blend until thoroughly combined. Weigh an empty container on a kitchen scale, then tare it to zero. Pour the blender mixture into the container and weigh. Add 0.5% by weight ascorbic acid and stir to combine.

ST. JOHNS SON

St. Augustine is America's oldest city and the home of datil peppers, the sweeter version of a habanero pepper. Daniel Cantliffe, professor of horticultural sciences at the University of Florida, finds that "St. Johns County is the only place on the planet this plant, the datil, has come from. We have looked around the planet; we can't find it anywhere else." The datil's Scoville score of 100,000–300,000 heat units belies its inherent sweetness, making it a great candidate for spirit infusions. The Floridian infuses local bourbon with datil peppers for this drink.

GLASSWARE: Rocks glass
GARNISH: Lemon wheel, smoked rosemary sprig, Bittercube
Blackstrap Bitters

- ¼ ripe peach
- ½ sprig fresh rosemary
- ¾ oz. fresh lemon juice
- 1½ oz. Datil-Infused Bourbon (see recipe)
- ½ oz. Basil-Infused Falernum (see recipe)
- ½ oz. orgeat
- ½ oz. Cynar

1. In a cocktail shaker tin, muddle the peach, rosemary, and lemon juice.
2. Add the remaining ingredients and ice and shake.

3. Strain the cocktail over a large ice cube into a rocks glass.

4. Smoke a sprig of rosemary with a smoking gun and add the sprig as a garnish, along with a lemon wheel and bitters.

BASIL-INFUSED FALERNUM: In a saucepan over high heat, bring 1 (750 ml) bottle Falernum and 1 cup whole fresh basil leaves to a boil. Cut the heat, let the mixture cool, then strain and rebottle the Falernum.

DATIL-INFUSED BOURBON: In a container, combine 1 (750 ml) bottle St. Augustine Florida Straight Bourbon and 3 datil peppers, sliced in half, and allow the infusion to sit for 10 minutes. Strain and rebottle the bourbon.

NOT SO BASIC BEE

This riff on the Bee's Knees creates the same refreshing experience as the original but with more complexity and the inclusion of local datil peppers for a little heat.

GLASSWARE: Coupe glass

GARNISH: 2 dashes lavender bitters, lemon twist

- 1½ oz. vodka
- 1 oz. Aperol
- 1 oz. grapefruit juice
- ¾ oz. fresh lime juice
- ½ oz. orange liqueur
- ½ oz. Strawberry-Datil Cordial (see recipe)

1. Combine all of the ingredients in a cocktail shaker with ice and shake vigorously.
2. Strain the cocktail into a coupe glass with pebble ice.
3. Garnish with lavender bitters and a lemon twist.

STRAWBERRY-DATIL CORDIAL: In a medium saucepan over medium heat, combine 1 cup strawberry puree, 1 cup sugar, 1 cup water, and ½ inch peeled, chopped fresh ginger and bring the mixture to a simmer. Add half a pinch Datil Dust (see recipe) and stir frequently. Zest ½ lime and ½ orange and squeeze the juices into the saucepan. Add ½ barspoon orange blossom water and bring the mixture to a boil, stirring. Turn off the heat, allow the cordial to cool, and strain and bottle it.

TYLER FAUST, THE CITIZEN

The Citizen in Alys Beach shines with its marine blue and mid-century modern brass interior. It boasts a wood-fired hearth, an eighteen-seat marble-inlaid bar, elegant glassware, and a twelve-seat raw bar with professional oyster shuckers. Overall, the place is buzzing with activity and grace.

Lead bartender Tyler Faust, whose team works closely with the kitchen, changes the The Citizen's cocktail menu seasonally. "I like to see what produce they have back there and what we can cross-utilize between the bar and the kitchen, making it a more cohesive guest experience from food to drink," Faust says.

SPRING TEA

The Citizen always has at least one cocktail on the menu that uses hand-shaved ice from the bar's traditional Japanese ice-shaving machine, even in winter. Bartender Landon Albright, who loves teas, started playing around with green tea and locally produced 30A Ciao Limoncello, trying to hit the right note with the shaved ice. Cathead Honeysuckle Vodka provided the perfect neutral spirit with floral notes. "We present it like a dessert, with the shaved green tea ice in a footed glass and the entire cocktail in a sidecar to pour over. It's really fresh and lemony, and as the cocktail melts the ice, it becomes this delicious boozy slushy," lead bartender Tyler Faust says.

GLASSWARE: Footed glass, sidecar

GARNISH: Lemon twist

- ½ oz. 30A Ciao Limoncello
- 1½ oz. Cathead Honeysuckle Vodka
- ½ oz. fresh lemon juice
- Green tea, frozen, as needed

1. Combine the limoncello, vodka, and lemon juice in a mixing glass.
2. Shave the frozen green tea into a footed glass.
3. Pour the limoncello mixture into a sidecar.
4. Garnish with a lemon twist.

CITIZENALYS.COM

FLEUR DE VIE

The Fleur de Vie takes inspiration from the spring blooms that blossom in northwest Florida starting in March—the lavender syrup, elderflower liqueur, and botanical gin together taste like spring in a glass. Tyler Faust drops a dried rosebud in as a final garnish to bring the theme home.

GLASSWARE: Nick & Nora glass

GARNISH: Dried rosebud

- 1½ oz. Nolet's Silver Gin
- ¾ oz. St-Germain Elderflower Liqueur
- ¾ oz. fresh lemon juice
- ½ oz. aquafaba
- ¼ oz. Dubonnet Rouge Grand Aperitif de France
- ¼ oz. Lavender Syrup (see recipe on page 114)
- 3 drops Saline Solution (see recipe on page 14)

1. Combine all of the ingredients in a cocktail shaker with ice and shake vigorously.
2. Double-strain the cocktail into a Nick & Nora glass.
3. Garnish with a dried rosebud.

MARGARITA VERDE

THE CITIZEN
20 MARK TWAIN LANE #101, ALYS BEACH

This Spicy Margarita take includes avocado syrup, which adds an unctuous mouthfeel to smooth out the spice.

GLASSWARE: Rocks glass

GARNISH: Jalapeño slice

- Tajín, for the rim
- 1½ oz. Jalapeño-Infused Tequila (see recipe)
- ½ oz. Ancho Reyes Verde Chile Poblano Liqueur
- 1 oz. Avocado Simple Syrup (see recipe)
- 1 oz. fresh lime juice

1. Wet the rim of a rocks glass with lime juice then dip the glass in Tajín to give it a rim.

2. Combine the remaining ingredients in a cocktail shaker with ice and shake vigorously.

3. Strain the cocktail over ice into the rimmed rocks glass.

4. Garnish with a slice of fresh jalapeño.

JALAPEÑO-INFUSED TEQUILA: In a container, combine 1 (750 ml) bottle tequila and 1 fresh jalapeño, sliced in half. Allow the infusion to sit for 15 to 20 minutes. Strain the tequila back into the bottle.

AVOCADO SIMPLE SYRUP: Add 1 quart Simple Syrup (see recipe on page 14) and ½ avocado to a blender and blend until thoroughly combined, about 1 minute.

AFTERNOON OLD FASHIONED

THE CITIZEN
20 MARK TWAIN LANE #101, ALYS BEACH

The Old Fashioned gets a new twist with this Japanese whiskey–based take. Cherry bitters bring a hit of sweetness and a layer of spice.

GLASSWARE: Rocks glass

GARNISH: Lemon peel, orange peel, Amarena cherry

- 1 oz. Suntory Whisky Toki
- 1 oz. Old Forester 86 Proof Bourbon
- ¼ oz. Simple Syrup (see recipe on page 14)
- 5 dashes Woodford Reserve Spiced Cherry Bitters

1. Combine all of the ingredients in a mixing glass and fill the glass with ice.
2. Stir until the cocktail is chilled and diluted.
3. Strain the cocktail over a large cube of ice into a rocks glass.
4. Garnish with a lemon peel, orange peel, and Amarena cherry.

JUSTIN LEVAUGHN, OTTO'S HIGH DIVE

Born and raised in Central Florida, environmentalist and outdoorsman Justin Levaughn strives to bring Florida's environments into the drinks he creates. "An avid surfer my entire life, I spend a lot of time beachside, but when there's not a lot of swell, I spend all my time off hiking among the Florida springs, kayaking, or exploring our river systems," he says. "I'm in tune with our lesser-known flora, fauna, and produce, and I love to incorporate that knowledge into my cocktails."

He worked his way up through the hospitality industry, but it was a visit to New York's Please Don't Tell bar that set him on his path in mixology, which eventually led to him being crowned the MICHELIN Guide Florida 2024 Exceptional Cocktail Award Winner for his work at Otto's.

FLORIDIAN SLIP

OTTO'S HIGH DIVE
2304 EAST ROBINSON STREET, ORLANDO

For those looking for a delicious take on a Margarita, Otto's High Dive co-owner Justin Levaughn serves you the Floridian Slip. "Some of the best produce we are known for in Florida is dehydrated to preserve its lifespan. I pull from that cache as needed to make the Florida Tea Syrup. The tea on its own is great as well," he says.

GLASSWARE: Rocks glass

GARNISH: Fresh mint sprig, Tajín-dusted orange slice

- 2 oz. blanco tequila
- ½ oz. Kalani Coconut Liqueur
- ¾ oz. Florida Tea Syrup (see recipe)
- ¾ oz. fresh lime juice

1. Combine all of the ingredients in a cocktail shaker tin with ice. Shake and strain into a rocks glass over pebble ice.

2. Garnish with a mint sprig and Tajín-dusted orange slice.

FLORIDA TEA SYRUP: Combine equal parts dried hibiscus flowers, rose hips, orange blossoms, dehydrated apples, dehydrated pineapples, and toasted coconut to make 1 cup dried tea mix. In a saucepan boil 4 cups water then steep the tea in the boiling water for 3 minutes. Turn the heat to low. Add 2 quarts unrefined sugar and simmer, stirring until the sugar is dissolved. Remove from heat and allow the syrup to cool. Strain and store in the refrigerator for up to 2 weeks.

PAHAYOKEE

OTTO'S HIGH DIVE
2304 EAST ROBINSON STREET, ORLANDO

Named after the original Seminole name for the Everglades, co-owner Justin Levaughn crafted this cocktail to visually resemble the Everglades, "with a mossy green surface and clear subsurface full of abundance, life, and flavor."

GLASSWARE: Nick & Nora glass

GARNISH: Nasturtium leaf, small Egyptian star flower

- 2 oz. Saint James Blanc Agricole 55°
- ¾ oz. Marie Brizard Yuzu Liqueur
- ¾ oz. Lime Acid Blend (see recipe)
- ½ oz. Citrus Oleo (see recipe)
- Barspoon Charred Fresno Pepper & Dill Oil (see recipe)

1. Combine all of the ingredients in a Nick & Nora glass and stir.
2. Garnish with a floated nasturtium leaf and a small Egyptian star flower.

CITRUS OLEO: Vacuum seal 1 quart superfine (caster) sugar, ½ quart water, 1 cup lime peels, and 1 oz. orange blossom water and allow the mixture to sit overnight at room temperature. Sous vide the oleo the next day at 145°F for 1 to 2 hours, or until the sugar is dissolved. Strain and cool.

CHARRED FRESNO PEPPER & DILL OIL: Tightly pack a blender halfway with fresh dill and fresh Italian parsley. Add 1 tablespoon sea salt, 6 Fresno peppers, grilled, and then fill the blender one-third of the way with a neutral oil, like avocado oil. Blend at a high speed until the oil has become hot enough to begin smoking. Stop the blender and strain the oil through a coffee filter. Keep refrigerated.

LIME ACID BLEND: In a glass or other nonreactive container, combine 260 grams water, 50 grams phosphoric solution (1.25%), 9 grams citric acid powder, 6 grams malic powder, 1 gram salt, and 0.2 grams tartaric powder and stir until the powders are dissolved. The acid blend is designed to mimic the acid profile of the key lime.

QUATFATHER

OTTO'S HIGH DIVE
2304 EAST ROBINSON STREET, ORLANDO

Native to China, kumquats and loquats tolerate Central Florida's cooler winters well and provide a smaller, tarter version of the orange found in groves around Florida.

GLASSWARE: Sling glass

GARNISH: Loquat leaves, 2 loquats, edible flower

- 1½ oz. Spanish gin
- ½ oz. Élixir Combier
- ¾ oz. Quat Cordial (see recipe)
- ¾ oz. fresh lemon juice
- Orange Blossom Absinthe Mist (see recipe)

1. Combine all of the ingredients in a cocktail shaker and shake.

2. Pour the cocktail over pebble ice into a sling glass.

3. Garnish with loquat leaves, 2 loquats, and an edible flower.

QUAT CORDIAL: Vacuum seal ½ cup dried kumquats, ½ cup chopped fresh loquats, 1 quart sugar, and ½ quart water and sous vide at 145°F for 2 hours. Strain the cordial and refrigerate it.

ORANGE BLOSSOM ABSINTHE MIST: In a container, stir together 2 oz. absinthe and 1 oz. orange blossom water and bottle the mixture in an atomizer.

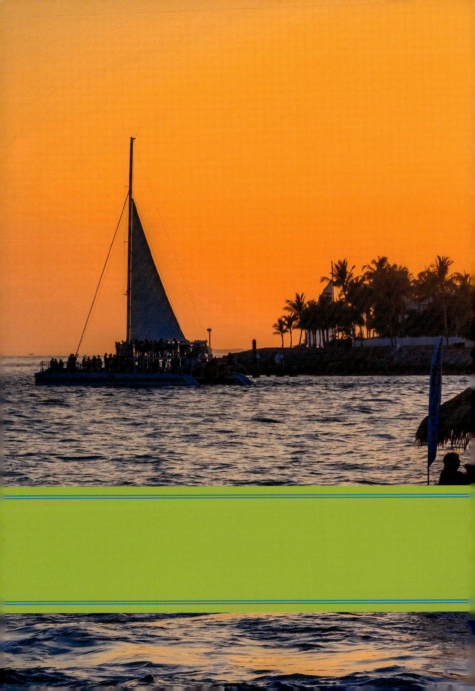

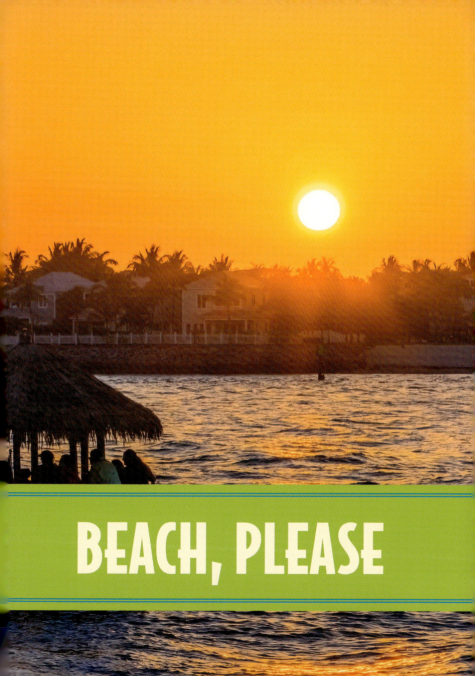

BEACH, PLEASE

ANDY MCKOSKI, CHIRINGO

Chiringo owner Andy McKoski found his mantra on a trip to Spain—keep it simple. When he opened in the fiercely independent beach town of Grayton Beach, that phrase served as the ethos underpinning the relaxed beach bar, where you are welcome whether you just rolled in off the beach in a bathing suit or are dressed for an evening out.

Andy started in hospitality at fifteen years old in the kitchen. By eighteen, he had moved to the bar. He paid his way through college tending bar, but because he had grown up in the hospitality business, Andy swore it would never be his career. After bouncing around corporate America, he came back to hospitality and opened his own restaurant. That led to many more restaurants and bars, and by the time he had racked up twelve, Andy needed a break. He left all that and went to Spain. "At their beach bars, you didn't get a choice of what flavor vodka you wanted. There was one vodka, one rum. They used fresh juices to flavor their drinks," McKoski says. He took that simplicity of execution, came back to the States, and opened his beach bar with three vodkas, one or two rums, one or two whiskeys, and one gin.

For McCoski, a great beach bar is about the connections you make. "I think of Hemingway in Key West, Penrod's on South Beach, AJ's in Destin. Places where you sit down at the bar and the CEO of Chevron might be sitting next to Jake, who rents out beach chairs, and they are talking like best friends. Because the best beach bars are never about what's going on outside the bar. You're just there, having a conversation. There's good music and the slightest smell of sunscreen and tanning oil. My childhood in South Florida was Coppertone-infused. The only thing I miss here on 30A is a marina—the smell of boat gas reminds me of being a kid."

KIMCHI BLOODY MARY

CHIRINGO
63 HOTZ AVENUE, GRAYTON BEACH

Bartender Tom Graham was never a fan of Bloody Marys. "The taste, the consistency, all of it was just not for me," he says. When he moved to Florida and took over the bar program at Chiringo, he was tasked with creating a drink for a Fourth of July parade. He came up with the Kimchi Bloody Mary. "I added a few more raw natural ingredients to dial in the flavor, and then a thought popped into my head—to use this vintage wine press to extract the flavor of the kimchi, natural ingredients, and spices. It was the answer—a more vegetal and Asian-influenced Bloody Mary, with a consistency more likened to a light pinot noir. It has all the flavor and none of the thickness," he says. Soon, his proprietary mix (Sully's) will be available for purchase, but for now, it resides only in the Chiringo well, ready to ease a morning hangover or just get the day started right.

GLASSWARE: 16 oz. cup

GARNISH: Baby corn, cucumber slice, bean sprouts

- 4 oz. Bloody Mary mix
- 2 oz. Tito's Handmade Vodka

1. Combine the ingredients in a mixing glass over ice and roll (see page 15 for the technique).
2. Garnish with a baby corn, a slice of cucumber, and bean sprouts.

HOTZ SUMMER

CHIRINGO
63 HOTZ AVENUE, GRAYTON BEACH

Height-of-season strawberries, tart lemonade, and fresh-from-the-garden mint brings a summery zest to this cocktail. This is one of bartender and partner Travis Matney's creations; he favors the brininess the vodka, from Distillery 98, adds to the mix.

GLASSWARE: 16 oz. cup

- **1 oz. sliced fresh strawberries**
- **4 to 5 mint leaves**
- **2 oz. Dune Laker Vodka**
- **3 oz. lemonade**
- **½ oz. soda water, to top**

1. Muddle the strawberries and mint in the bottom of a cup. Add ice to fill the cup.

2. Add the vodka and lemonade, then pour the cup into a cocktail shaker and shake vigorously.

3. Strain the cocktail into the cup then top with soda water.

BILLY OCEAN

CHIRINGO
63 HOTZ AVENUE, GRAYTON BEACH

When Chiringo bartender and partner Travis Matney was tasked with creating a delicious drink that felt refreshing, the Billy Ocean came to life. Chiringo owner Andy McKoski, giving the background for his assignment, adds, "I grew up in Miami. Instead of doing a Bushwhacker or Piña Colada, I wanted something that had fresh mango, fresh pineapple, ginger, and a different vibe than the typical frozen drink."

GLASSWARE: 16 oz. plastic cup

GARNISH: ½ oz. Myers's Rum Original Dark, mango slice

- **2 oz. Captain Morgan Original Spiced Rum**
- **2 oz. fresh pineapple juice**
- **2 oz. fresh mango juice**
- **½ oz. ginger syrup**

1. Add all of the ingredients to a cup filled with ice and stir.
2. Add a floater of ½ oz. Myers's Rum Original Dark. Garnish with a mango slice.

KENTUCKY BUCK

NORTH BEACH SOCIAL
24200 US-331, SANTA ROSA BEACH

Bartender Erick Castro, inspired by seasonal strawberries and the lack of bourbon-based cocktail recipes in the books he was reading, created the Kentucky Buck in 2008 at San Francisco's Bourbon & Branch. Jennifer Summers, manager of North Beach Social, wanted to put something on the menu that spoke to the colors of the sunsets over the Choctawhatchee Bay. "The sunset here has a complex variety of colors with the orange, purple, and yellow, and the port barrel bourbon we use adds some backbone to the fruit flavors," she says. "It's a drink for when the sun slips on another day."

GLASSWARE: 12 oz. cup

GARNISH: Lime wedge

- **Fresh strawberries, to taste**
- **Dash lemon juice**
- **Dash bitters**
- **2 oz. Angel's Envy Kentucky Straight Bourbon**
- **Ginger beer, to top**

1. Muddle the strawberries, lemon juice, and bitters in a 12 oz. cup.

2. Add ice and the bourbon. Top with ginger beer.

3. Garnish with a lime wedge.

SPICY PALOMA

NORTH BEACH SOCIAL
24200 US-331, SANTA ROSA BEACH

This take on the classic Mexican cocktail adds extra layers of grapefruit with the vodka and the soda, plus some jalapeño kick.

GLASSWARE: 12 oz. cup

GARNISH: Lime wedge, mint sprig

- 1 oz. Deep Eddy Ruby Red Grapefruit Vodka
- 1 oz. Patrón Reposado
- Jalapeño slices, to taste
- Fever-Tree Sparkling Pink Grapefruit, to top
- Grapefruit juice, to top

1. In a 12 oz. cup, muddle the vodka, tequila, and jalapeños.
2. Fill the cup with ice then top with the soda and grapefruit juice.
3. Garnish with a lime wedge and a mint sprig.

TROPICAL MOJITO

NORTH BEACH SOCIAL
24200 US-331, SANTA ROSA BEACH

Manager Jennifer Summers wanted to put a Mojito on the menu at North Beach Social, but she didn't want the standard version. In this riff, Summers uses a tropical rum with notes of pineapple, coconut, and guava, transforming it into the ultimate summertime drink. Agave nectar takes the place of the usual sugar to create a lighter, less sweet flavor.

GLASSWARE: 12 oz. cup

GARNISH: Lime wedge, mint sprig

- **2 oz. Bacardí Tropical Flavored Rum**
- **½ oz. agave nectar**
- **¼ oz. fresh lime juice**
- **Mint leaves, to taste**
- **Soda water, to top**

1. In a 12 oz. cup, muddle the rum, agave nectar, lime juice, and mint.

2. Fill the cup with ice and top with soda water.

3. Garnish with a lime wedge and a mint sprig.

WASTED WHALE

NORTH BEACH SOCIAL
24200 US-331, SANTA ROSA BEACH

Honoring the large mural of a Rice's whale found at North Beach Social, the Wasted Whale blends a number of flavors together smoothly. "It's got a great harmony of floral and citrus flavors, and the guava adds that balance of sweet and sour," says manager Jennifer Summers. "Soda water at the end keeps it light, refreshing, and perfect for the hot Florida sun."

GLASSWARE: 12 oz. cup

GARNISH: Lime wedge

- **1½ oz. Gray Whale Gin**
- **½ oz. guava juice**
- **¼ oz. fresh lemon juice**
- **¼ oz. fresh lime juice**
- **Dash Simple Syrup (see recipe on page 14)**
- **Soda water, to top**

1. Combine all of the ingredients, except for the soda water, in a cocktail shaker and shake.
2. Pour the cocktail into a 12 oz. cup filled with ice, then top with soda water.
3. Garnish with a lime wedge.

SLOPPY JOE'S

201 DUVAL STREET, KEY WEST

A hundred years ago, Key West native Joe Russell was not only Ernest Hemingway's boat pilot and fishing companion, but he was also a rum-runner, illegally onshoring rum during Prohibition under cover of night. He went legal after the end of Prohibition and it was thanks to Hemingway that the name, inspired by a bar in Havana that Papa liked, stuck.

The great author immortalized Joe Russell in his novel *To Have and Have Not*. Russell served as the model for Freddy, the owner of Freddy's bar and captain of the Queen Conch in the book. In 1937, the rent for Sloppy Joe's went up, and Russell and his patrons relocated the bar to its new location—except for the men's urinal, which Hemingway took to his home a few blocks away, where it was converted into a fountain for his six-toed cats.

Sloppy Joe's is often tourists' first stop in Key West. Every New Year's Eve, Sloppy Joe's bartenders drop a conch to ring in the New Year in the Conch Republic.

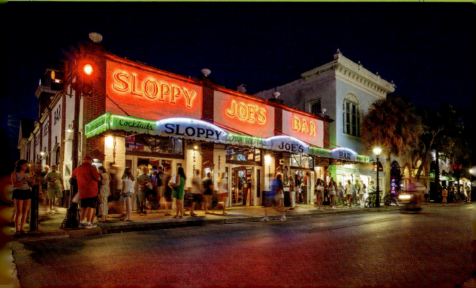

THE 201

SLOPPY JOE'S BAR
201 DUVAL STREET, KEY WEST

Created by bartender Chris Agard, The 201 celebrates the landing spot for Sloppy Joe's Bar after a late-night move prompted by a hike in rent on the original location. The rum is crafted especially for the bar by Papa's Pilar Distillery. You can substitute Papa's Pilar Flagship Blonde Rum or another light-colored rum of your choice.

GLASSWARE: 12 oz. plastic cup

GARNISH: Maraschino cherry

- 1 oz. Sloppy Joe's Blonde Reserve Rum
- ½ oz. Licor 43
- Pineapple juice, to top

1. Fill a 12 oz. cup with ice, then add the rum and liqueur.
2. Fill the cup with pineapple juice and roll the cocktail to mix the ingredients properly.
3. Garnish with a maraschino cherry.

SLOPPY GINGER

SLOPPY JOE'S BAR
201 DUVAL STREET, KEY WEST

Touted as one of the best Mule-style cocktails on Key West, the Sloppy Ginger keeps it simple with just three ingredients. Break out the classic copper mule cups for this one when making it at home.

GLASSWARE: Copper cup

- 1½ oz. Ketel One Vodka
- Ginger beer, to top
- Juice of 1 lime wedge

1. Fill a cup with ice, then add the vodka.
2. Fill the cup with ginger beer. Squeeze a lime wedge over top and stir.

PROHIBITION PUNCH

SLOPPY JOE'S BAR
201 DUVAL STREET, KEY WEST

A nod to the classic Prohibition Punch, mixed up illicitly in the 1920s, this riff subs in the king of spirits in Key West, rum, for the traditional whiskey. Sloppy Joe's uses a specially made rum from Hemingway Distillery (formerly Papa's Pilar), but you can use any light-colored rum of your choice.

GLASSWARE: 12 oz. plastic cup

GARNISH: Maraschino cherry

- 1 oz. Sloppy Joe's Blonde Reserve Rum
- ½ oz. Papa's Pilar Flagship Dark Rum
- Splash grenadine
- Orange juice, to top
- Pineapple juice, to top

1. Fill a 12 oz. cup with ice, then add the rums and grenadine.
2. Top with equal parts orange juice and pineapple juice until the cup is filled. Then roll the cocktail to mix the ingredients properly.

SOUTHERNMOST MUTINY

SLOPPY JOE'S BAR
201 DUVAL STREET, KEY WEST

S loppy Joe's sticks to its island ethos with this drink, which employs a unique vodka crafted from breadfruit. Breadfruit is not only a superfood, but the trees sequester tons of carbon that helps mitigate global warming. Breadfruit is better for the soil than commonly distilled crops like corn and potatoes. Produced on the Island of St. Croix, Mutiny Island Vodka comes from a zero-waste facility and pledges to practice only sustainable sourcing and distilling.

GLASSWARE: 12 oz. plastic cup

- **Sprig fresh mint**
- **Lemon wedge**
- **1½ oz. Mutiny Island Vodka Roots**
- **Lemonade, to top**
- **Club soda, to top**

1. In a 12 oz. cup, muddle the mint and lemon wedge, then fill the cup with ice.

2. Pour the vodka into the cup then top with lemonade and a splash of club soda.

3. Roll the drink to mix the ingredients properly.

HONEY, IT'S SUMMER

PREZZO
5560 NORTH MILITARY TRAIL #100, BOCA RATON

What says summer more than bright citrus, fresh basil, and a touch of local honey? This is smooth-drinking summertime in a glass. At Prezzo, everything from the kitchen to the bar is prepared with the highest quality ingredients sourced locally and from Italy.

GLASSWARE: Rocks glass

GARNISH: Basil sprig

- Basil sprig
- 2 oz. Johnnie Walker Black Label
- 1 oz. fresh lemon juice
- 1 oz. Simple Syrup (see recipe on page 14)
- ½ oz. honey

1. In a cocktail shaker tin, muddle the basil. Then add the remaining ingredients with ice and shake.
2. Strain the cocktail over a big ice cube into a rocks glass.
3. Garnish with a fresh basil sprig.

POOLSIDE PASSION FRUIT

PREZZO
5560 NORTH MILITARY TRL #100, BOCA RATON

This cocktail carries the smoky undertones of Kentucky bourbon but offers a refreshing Florida twist, with passion fruit liqueur. And it's topped with sparkling wine, which is never a bad idea.

✳

GLASSWARE: Rocks glass

GARNISH: Skewer of orange, lime, and maraschino cherry

- 1 oz. Angel's Envy Kentucky Straight Bourbon
- 1 oz. passion fruit liqueur
- ½ oz. vanilla vodka
- ½ oz. fresh lime juice
- ½ oz. Simple Syrup (see recipe on page 14)
- Prosecco, to top

1. Combine all of the ingredients, except for the prosecco, in a cocktail shaker and shake.
2. Strain the cocktail into a rocks glass over fresh ice.
3. Top with prosecco and garnish with a skewer of orange, lime, and maraschino cherry.

SUMMER BLUES SPRITZER

CORVINA
110 PLAZA REAL SOUTH, BOCA RATON

Created by head bartender Oscar Garcia, the Summer Blues Spritzer takes advantage of two fresh Florida products: blueberries, at their height of ripeness, and mint that grows like a weed across the state.

GLASSWARE: Collins glass
GARNISH: Mint sprig, blueberries

- 6 blueberries
- Mint, to taste
- 1½ oz. Bushmills The Original Irish Whiskey
- ¾ oz. fresh lemon juice
- ¾ oz. Simple Syrup (see recipe on page 14)
- ½ oz. lychee liqueur
- ½ oz. Stoli Blueberry Vodka
- Club soda, to top

1. Muddle the blueberries and mint in a shaker tin.
2. Add the remaining ingredients, except for the club soda, and ice, close the shaker, and shake well.
3. Pour the cocktail into a collins glass and top with club soda.

SUMMER BREEZE

MAGIC 13 BREWING CO.
340 NORTHAST 61ST STREET, MIAMI

A 1980s cocktail, The Sea Breeze, serves as inspiration for this drink with its vodka base and grapefruit juice. But then it veers off from there in citrusy, spicy, bubbly directions.

GLASSWARE: Collins glass
GARNISH: Dehydrated orange slice

- Tajín, for the rim
- 2 oz. vodka
- 2 oz. grapefruit juice
- ½ oz. orange syrup
- ¼ oz. fresh lime juice
- Splash Topo Chico Sparkling Mineral Water, to top

1. Wet the rim of a collins glass with lime juice then dip the glass in Tajín to give it a rim.

2. Combine the remaining ingredients, except for the mineral water, in a mixing glass with ice and stir.

3. Strain the cocktail into the rimmed collins glass and fill with ice.

4. Top with sparkling water and garnish with a dehydrated orange slice.

FLORIDA'S LEGENDARY DIVES & BEACH BARS

Have you even been to Florida if you haven't lifted a drink at one of these institutions?

FLORA-BAMA
17401 PERDIDO KEY DRIVE, PENSACOLA

On Perdido Key, on the line separating Florida and Alabama, sits the bar that launched a television series, inspired songs by legends like Jimmy Buffett, and appeared in books like John Grisham's *The Pelican Brief*.

The saga started in 1962, when Florida gave Alabama two miles of beachfront land on which to build the Perdido Pass Bridge. The Tam-

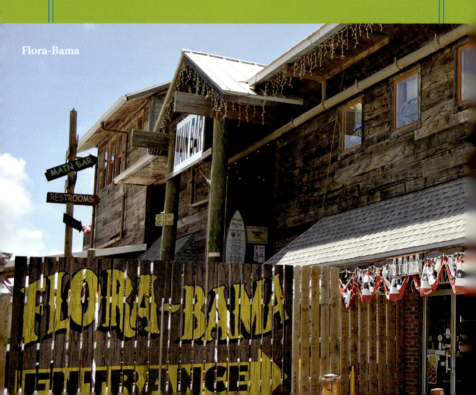

Flora-Bama

pary family (father Ted, sons Connie and Tony) built a small bar and package store on the state line in 1964, even though the Alabama side was a dry county, and the Florida side served.

What began as one of the only businesses on the key grew as traffic bloomed on the new highway. Today it is Flora-Bama, forming a "No-Shoes Nation" with the Yacht Club, Ole River Grill, and the slightly bigger original bar. It is filled with hanging dollar bills, photos of the famous musicians who have played in its hallowed halls, and clotheslines strung along the ceiling with collections of bras left behind.

You never know who might show up—there was once an impromptu Kenny Chesney concert on the beach—or what you might find, but it is always a good time, and the drinks are always flowing. Their signature drink, the Bushwacker, is a doozy, especially for a frozen drink. It looks and tastes like a mashup of the best White Russian and chocolate milkshake you've ever had, but beware, she's strong.

THE SANDSHAKER LOUNGE
731 PENSACOLA BEACH BOULEVARD, PENSACOLA BEACH

Only a few bars can say they were put on the map with one drink, but the Sandshaker Lounge can. When Linda Taylor opened this place in 1973, she didn't know that a drink idea she brought back from vacationing on St. Thomas would make her bar famous—and start a battle among beach bars around the Gulf Coast for bragging rights about who made it first. The Bushwacker, originally conceived by bartender Angie Congliaro and restaurant manager Tom Brokamp at the Ship's Store and Sapphire Pub on St. Thomas, spread like wildfire across St. Thomas and the Virgin Islands. Most people agree the Sandshaker Lounge had it on the menu first. They even have a festival devoted to the drink in August every year.

LE TUB
1100 NORTH OCEAN DRIVE, HOLLYWOOD

Across the street from Hollywood Beach, a collection of clawfoot tubs, driftwood, and washed-ashore bric-a-brac draws curious visitors in, but it is not a vintage store or souvenir shop; it is the legendary dive bar Le Tub. The burger recipe hasn't changed since they opened in 1975. Russel T. Kohuth, Le Tub's founder, transformed the former gas station with objects he scouted on his daily jogs. Local lifeguards pitched in with quirky treasures they found washed ashore in exchange for beers. Over the years, regular customers have donated their own mementos and nautical paraphernalia to the walls and ceilings. You can even boat up to Le Tub and sit on the water at tables crafted from sun-bleached dock boards from marinas all over the United States. So come as you are, and get one of their legendary burgers and a refreshing cocktail to sip while you watch the sunset over the bay.

STINKY'S BAIT SHACK
5994 WEST COUNTY ROAD 30A, SANTA ROSA BEACH

Driving by, you might think this is a tackle-and-bait shop. And you would be right. But they also have cold beer, wine, liquor, and frozen Daiquiris to take to the beach. At night, the rustic venue transforms into a haven for live music. This spot checks all the boxes for a great Florida beach bar—they prioritize fun, you always feel comfortable even if you just rolled in off the beach, local bands are on the stage, and the drinks are delicious but not pretentious. Draught beer is popular, but everybody comes for the Daiquiris. Inspired by their New Orleans roots, owner Jim Richard developed a Daiquiri program featuring their signature drink, The Stink Juice. According to corporate chef and managing partner Todd Misener, the drink developed out of necessity. "Back when flavored vodka hit the scene and was all but free, we had a lot of backstock of a certain brand that needed to be sold. The Stink Juice was born," he said. All of the Daiquiris, including The Stink Juice, are made with fresh juices.

THE DAIQUIRI DECK
5250 OCEAN BOULEVARD, SARASOTA

As Troy Syprett sipped on Daiquiris in Key West in 1993, an idea came to him: a Daiquiri shack on Siesta Key would be the perfect end to a day spent on the beach. Six months later, the Sarasota native opened The Daiquiri Deck. The appeal of rows of Daiquiri machines pumping out a variety of flavors, including their first recipe, the Deck Diesel, against the backdrop of fiery sunsets became an instant success. All drinks are made with sugarcane instead of high-fructose corn syrup. They also have Floridian bites like conch fritters and classic tacos that have been on the menu since 1993. If you're feeling adventurous, order "The Best One," a bartender's choice option, for a delicious surprise.

PETE'S BAR
117 FIRST STREET, NEPTUNE BEACH

Thought to be haunted, featured in John Grisham's novel *The Brethren*, and owned by the same family for over eight decades, this Neptune Beach dive bar was also the first bar to legally open in Duval County after Prohibition was repealed. The bar came before the founding of Neptune Beach in 1931. Peter Jensen opened Jensen's Market in the 1920s, and that evolved into the neighborhood watering hole, Pete's Bar, in 1933. Not much has changed since the early days. Pool and ping-pong tables have their place, the bar still throws a Thanksgiving bash that attracts thousands, and memorabilia from the last nine decades fills the space. Nancy Jensen, Peter's granddaughter, once said, "I had one man walk in the door and say, 'Thank God.' And I said, 'Why are you saying that, sir?' He said, 'I haven't been to this beach for forty years. Everything has changed but Pete's.'"

MAC'S CLUB DEUCE
222 14TH STREET, MIAMI BEACH

The bar scene in Miami is robust, including dive bars, but one remains a favorite among locals and visitors alike, Mac's Club Deuce. Back in the pastel 1980s, *Miami Vice* used the space as a filming location and lined the interior with pink and green neon. They also threw their cast parties here. In 2010, *Playboy* named it one of America's best dive bars. Anthony Bourdain declared it one of his favorite spots in the world. It opened in 1933 as Club Deuce. In 1964, bar regular Mac Klein purchased it and kept it the same over the decades. They have a full bar, but it is the cold beer, conversations with strangers, and occasional games of pool that you come for.

MS NEWBY'S
8711 THOMAS DRIVE, PANAMA CITY BEACH

In 1975, Melva and David Newby added to their growing cluster of businesses on Thomas Drive. What initially started as Newby's Trading Company in 1972—a gas station, beach supply, and grocery store—has become an iconic Panama City Beach bar. They have live music, karaoke, pool tables, but what everybody goes for is their signature drink, the Hunch Punch. They've added on to the original building over the years and, as hurricanes have stormed through, have expanded the package store and opened a satellite location in the curve off Thomas Drive, but one thing doesn't change: you can't say you've been to PCB until you've been to Ms Newby's and had a Hunch Punch. And bonus, you can get one at their drive-through, like fast food but more potent.

Le Tub

REEF RUNNER

THE DAIQUIRI DECK
5250 OCEAN BOULEVARD, SARASOTA

Tucked into Siesta Village, just over the bridge from Sarasota, an open-air beach bar with a line of Daiquiri machines, bright orange-and-green decor, and toes-in-the-sand seating has been pumping out refreshing frozen drinks since 1993. That's when local surfer Troy Syprett opened The Daiquiri Deck so he had a place to end the perfect day on the waves, where friends could gather, enjoy aocean breeze, and watch the sunset while sipping, yes, Daiquiris. The Mango Daiquiri here comes from the batch ice daiquri machine, but you can use your blender to make your favorite recipe.

GLASSWARE: Hurricane glass

GARNISH: ¼ oz. Papa's Pilar Flagship Dark Rum, orange slice

- 4 oz. pineapple juice
- 3 oz. frozen mango Daiquiri

- 2 oz. Papa's Pilar Flagship Blonde Rum
- ¼ oz. fresh lime juice

1. Combine all of the ingredients in a cocktail shaker with ice and shake.

2. Strain the cocktail into a hurricane glass filled with ice.

3. Garnish with a float of rum and an orange slice.

THE BUSHWACKER

THE SANDSHAKER LOUNGE
731 PENSACOLA BEACH BOULEVARD,
PENSACOLA BEACH

The Sandshaker Lounge has served more than two million Bush-wackers in the past fifty years. They mix them in a five-gallon bucket that goes into the frozen drink machines. They're made daily, and each batch makes about twenty-eight cocktails. This recipe serves two.

GLASSWARE: Plastic cups

GARNISH: Freshly grated nutmeg, mint sprig, pineapple wedge

- 4 oz. Coco López Cream of Coconut
- 4 oz. half-and-half
- 2 oz. Kahlúa
- 1 oz. Bacardí Superior White Rum
- 1 oz. white crème de cocoa

1. Combine all of the ingredients in a blender with 2 cups ice and blend until smooth.
2. Pour the cocktail into the cups and garnish with nutmeg, a mint sprig, and a pineapple wedge.

TOASTED PIÑA COLADA

LE TUB
1100 NORTH OCEAN DRIVE, HOLLYWOOD

The toasted coconut flakes add a hint of warmth to this take on the Piña Colada while the Amarena cherry, unlike its sweeter cousin, the maraschino cherry, imparts a bit of sour flavor, balancing the sweetness of the other ingredients.

GLASSWARE: 12 oz. plastic cup

GARNISH: Toasted coconut flakes, Amarena cherry

- **2 oz. Caribbean rum**
- **2 oz. Coco López Cream of Coconut**
- **2 oz. pineapple juice**
- **¼ oz. fresh lime juice**

1. Combine all of the ingredients in a blender with a large scoop of ice and blend until smooth.
2. Pour the cocktail into a cup and garnish with toasted coconut flakes and an Amarena black cherry.

MEASUREMENT CONVERSIONS

	1 dash		0.625 ml
	4 dashes		2.5 ml
	1 teaspoon		5 ml
¼ oz.			7.5 ml
⅓ oz.	2 teaspoons		10 ml
½ oz.	3 teaspoons	1 tablespoon	15 ml
⅔ oz.	4 teaspoons		20 ml
¾ oz.			22.5 ml
$^{17}/_{20}$ oz.			25 ml
1 oz.		2 tablespoons	30 ml
1½ oz.		3 tablespoons	45 ml
1¾ oz.			52.5 ml
2 oz.	4 tablespoons	¼ cup	60 ml
8 oz.		1 cup	250 ml
16 oz.	1 pint	2 cups	500 ml
24 oz.		3 cups	750 ml
32 oz.	1 quart	4 cups	1 liter (1,000 ml)

Acknowledgments

When I was writing this book, two spirits guided me: my father and my great-grandmother.

My father, Orin Rivers, who was taken from this world far too young, taught me to believe in myself always, to appreciate good food and drink, and how to move through this world with joy and kindness. He performed his rendition of the cowardly lion from *The Wizard of Oz* to help me go to sleep, filled my life with music, and taught me that camping was never complete without a breakfast of creamed chipped beef on toast, hot off the campfire grill.

My great-grandmother, Gertrude Stewart, who everybody, including me, called Nanny, taught me how to make dandelion wine and buttermilk donut sailors on her farm in Highgate, Vermont. Her dedication to living off the land, welcoming everybody into her home, and her encyclopedic knowledge of plants, herbs, and flavor inspired my career in hospitality.

I could not have written this book without my husband, who carted me around the state as we drank cocktails and immersed ourselves in the imbibing culture of Florida and helped me draft the rules for "Drinking Like a Floridian." Gratitude also goes out to my children, Dylan and Olivia, who encourage me to be fearless and soak up every moment of life.

And last, to the bartenders, cocktail historians, and hospitality professionals who generously shared their knowledge and passion with me, this book would not exist without you.

About the Author

Carrie Honaker writes about Florida, from Perdido Key to Key West and all parts in between. She's not sure where she will land next, but it will involve messy eating, a boozy Daiquiri, and finding the local dive bar. She has hauled oyster cages off Florida's Forgotten Coast, distilled raki with farmers on Crete, explored secret convent cookie windows in Spain, made guavaberry liqueur with a seventh-generation distiller on St. Maarten, and walked the streets of Spinalonga with a Greek historian. She writes the stories of the people and places she meets traveling across the globe. Her work appears regularly in print and online at *Travel + Leisure*, *Food & Wine*, *Southern Living*, *Bon Appétit*, *Condé Nast Traveler*, *Wine Enthusiast*, *Fodor's Travel*, *Afar*, and more. At home, Carrie leans into writing about the quirkier side of Florida, the farmers, distillers, and small batch makers around the Sunshine State, and initiatives to preserve historic art and architecture. She's also probably posting cute cat pictures or planning her next trip to Greece.

Image Credits

Pages 23, 25, 26, 29, 30 Michael Pisarri; 51 (bottom left) Anthony Nader - 52 Chefs; 61, 63, 65 Pablo Gabes; 67, 69, 71, Ashley Horowitz; 73 Sarah Annay; 80 Julie Soefer; 83, 86 Otto Development; 88 (inset), 88–89, 91, 92, 95 Melissa Macarelle; 105 (inset) The Workmans; 113, 115, 116 Melissa Lushbaugh of South Made Marketing; 126, 131 Chris Trull; 129 Kris Holman; 132, 135 Camera & Flask Photography; 138–139, 140, 143, 144, 147, 148, 151 A.J. Galecki; 153 (bottom left) Sean Pozin; 180, 200, 203 Amanda Olivero; 183, 186, 189 Action Studios; 190, 191 Michael Booini; 193 (top) Visit Jacksonville; 204, 206, 212 John Revisky; 205, 209, 211 Jacob Lesitsky; 215 Jimmy Fashner; 216, 219 Karen Culp Photography; 221, 225 Megan Monzo; 227, 228 Genie McNally; 230 Katie DeSantis; 232 Landon Albright-Floyd; 237, 239, 241, 243 Justin Levaughn; 247, 250 Savvibelle Photography LLC; 252 Chryseis Golden Photography;

Pages 1, 3, 4–5, 6, 9, 17, 20–21, 76–77, 102–103, 156–157, 178–179, 244–245 used under official license from Shutterstock.com.

Page 12 courtesy of the State Library and Archives of Florida.

Page 11 courtesy of Wikimedia Commons.

Page 79 courtesy of the Library of Congress.

All other images courtesy of the respective bars, restaurants, and interviewees.

INDEX

—About Cider Mill Press Book Publishers—

Good ideas ripen with time. From seed to harvest, Cider Mill Press brings fine reading, information, and entertainment together between the covers of its creatively crafted books. Our Cider Mill bears fruit twice a year, publishing a new crop of titles each spring and fall.

"Where Good Books Are Ready for Press"
501 Nelson Place
Nashville, Tennessee 37214
cidermillpress.com

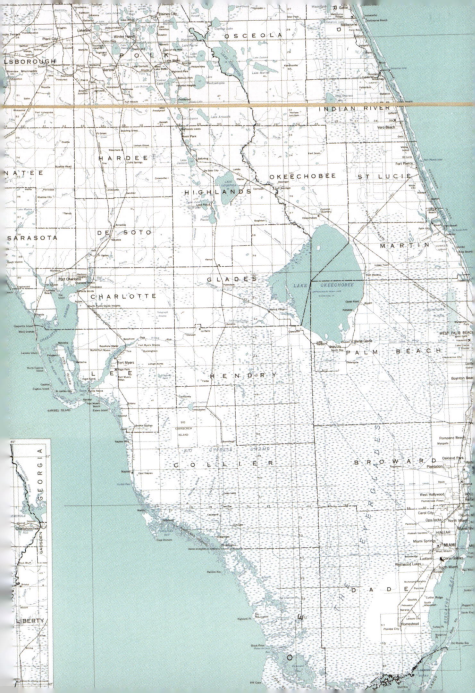

UNITED STATES
DEPARTMENT OF THE INTERIOR
GEOLOGICAL SURVEY

STATE OF FLORIDA

Scale 1:500,000
1 inch equals approximately 8 miles

Datum is mean sea level

Compiled, edited, and published by the Geological Survey.   1927 North American datum
Lambert conformal conic projection based on standard parallels 24° and 31½°

LEGEND

⊙ State capital
※ County seat
○ City, town, or village
✕ Scheduled service of port
▭ Built-up area shown for towns over 10,000 population
Private survey

SOURCE DATA

U. S. Dept. of the Interior–Geological Survey topographic maps

U. S. Dept. of the Army–Corps of Engineers topographic maps

BASE MAP

POPULATION KEY

MIAMI	more than 100,000
PENSACOLA	50,000 to 100,000
Ocala	25,000 to 50,000
Valparaiso	5,000 to 25,000
Gretna	less than 5,000

Population estimated by size of letters

FOR SALE BY U.S. GEOLOGICAL SURVEY, WASHINGTON, D. C. 20242
COMPILED IN 1962
EDITION OF 1967